The Relevance of History

The Relevance of History

by

Gordon Connell-Smith

and

Howell A. Lloyd

HEINEMANN EDUCATIONAL BOOKS
LONDON

Heinemann Educational Books Ltd
LONDON EDINBURGH MELBOURNE TORONTO
JOHANNESBURG NEW DELHI SINGAPORE
AUCKLAND IBADAN HONG KONG
NAIROBI KUALA LUMPUR

ISBN 0 435 32805 0

First published 1972

Published by
Heinemann Educational Books Ltd
48 Charles Street, London W1X 8AH
Printed in Great Britain by Morrison & Gibb Ltd
London and Edinburgh

Contents

to Wendy and Gaynor

Introduction

THIS book suggests that historians are faced today with two alternatives: either they establish the relevance of their subject or the study of history will decline. The reader, whether he is an historian or not, may be surprised by such a suggestion. For he appears to be surrounded by evidence that history is thriving. More history books than ever before are being bought, and some are best sellers; increasing numbers of people are deriving pleasure from our historical heritage, visiting monuments, museums, stately homes, and so on. Historical presentations on television enjoy great success; the same medium shows a seemingly endless number of historical films. Of course, very little of this amounts to serious historical study. But more seriously, history is widely taught in our schools and universities. A great many people have 'O' and 'A' level passes in the subject, and there are large numbers of history graduates. History seems to be part of the established order of things. Taken altogether, this surely is a very satisfactory state of affairs for the professional historians: the academics who practise history in our universities.

But being part of the established order of things is no guarantee of immunity from decline, especially in an age of rapid change. No one should be more aware of this than historians. Recently there has been a growing demand from young people – the age-group which society has been unprecedentedly eager to educate – that their education should be 'relevant': that is to say, it should have a clear and immediate bearing upon their current interests and aspirations. This demand is part of a general challenge to 'the establishment' and a manifestation of what is loosely called 'the generation gap'. Not surprisingly, academics generally have reacted unfavourably to it on the traditionally hallowed grounds that an academic subject is studied 'for its own sake'. Professional historians, by both nature and training a conservative group, advance this argument, and direct particular criticism at those who, they allege, seek the immediate applicability of historical 'lessons' to current problems.

Of course, demands for immediate relevance often are unreasoning. But professional historians would be extremely unwise to answer them with an equally unthinking dismissal of relevance as a proper matter for consideration in relation to their subject. For the challenge is much more serious, and their own position very much weaker, than they realise. History has been rendered particularly vulnerable by the insistence of professional historians that the study of the past should be deliberately divorced from the present and from the problems of contemporary society. The place of history in our schools and universities is already threatened by the growth of other disciplines – such as sociology – which claim to have direct relevance to society's present needs and problems. Professional historians are facing a growing challenge from their own students, who are impatient of vague answers to their questions regarding the value of their studying history for several years at university. What does such study contribute to their intellectual development? How does it prepare them for their future lives in society? Will it merely equip them to teach history in their turn and, if so, what benefits will they confer upon the pupils with whom they themselves will deal? These are legitimate questions, which will be asked increasingly often as greater numbers of young people receive higher education and more and more history graduates emerge into society.

The challenge is legitimate, above all, for a reason which professional historians appear to overlook. Regarding themselves primarily as scholars, they forget that they exist in their present numbers only because of history's presumed relevance as a medium of education. In other words, their primary social function is to teach students within a system of higher education. Thus we come to the main point. The 'relevance' with which we are concerned in this book is first and foremost the relevance of history as a medium of education; and we interpret 'education' to embrace both formal education in educational institutions, and educating laymen to a greater understanding of the contemporary issues and problems that directly concern them. The authors maintain that history in our schools and universities must be relevant to the intellectual development of the young people who study it, and thus to the wider needs and purposes of society, which supports it. It is our contention that history at present is studied and taught in a way that serves the interests of scholarship – *as professional historians interpret this* – rather than those of education; which means, in practice, the interests of the professional historians rather than those of the students whom society entrusts them to teach. This situation we regard as unjustifiable and likely to prove untenable.

The authors welcome the challenge. We believe it will compel a long overdue analysis of the way in which historians go about their work, both as scholars and as educators. Both roles are involved. We shall demonstrate how professional historians project into their work as teachers their approach to historical scholarship – with unfortunate results which call into question the validity of that approach itself. Professional historians, enjoyably probing their small sectors of the frontiers of knowledge, have lost sight of broader issues and goals. With their increasing specialisation, they have little to say to any but a few of their colleagues, let alone educated laymen: a category which includes all of their students except the handful who will themselves become professional historians. They have adopted an approach to history which involves their trying to divorce the past from the present, and themselves from society and its insistent problems. This preoccupation with analysing 'the past' as quite distinct from 'the present' – rather than with establishing a meaningful relationship between past and present situations – we judge to be quite misguided, and deleterious to the historian's work as both scholar and educator. By contrast we believe in the relevance of history owing chiefly to its unique capacity to promote in those who study it qualities of judgement in relation to complex and changing problems in human society. In other words, we affirm that the study of history, properly pursued, has particular relevance for society in an age of unprecedented change.

Our purpose in writing this book is to stimulate a *public* debate on the role of history as a medium of education. Professional historians are involved because theirs is the greatest responsibility for the way history is studied and taught. But they are only one of the interested parties. The teachers of history in our schools and colleges also are deeply involved. Not only were many of them trained by the professional historians, but university approaches

to the subject greatly influence the way history is taught elsewhere, and determine the materials at the disposal of its teachers.
For if documents are the raw materials for professional historians,
what the latter make of them (in terms of the books they write)
forms the raw materials for the teachers in the schools and
colleges.[1] But we seek a much wider audience still, embracing
not only all those who study history, but even those who read it
for pleasure and want to know 'what the whole thing is about'.
Nor is this all. During the discussion we shall indicate (albeit
briefly) the significance of this debate about history for the wider
issues involved in education today. In short, then, we address our
argument to all those interested not only in history, but also in
education.

Our argument is developed in four main chapters and a
conclusion. In the first chapter, Lloyd surveys the historical
background to the present situation. He analyses the ways in
which men have studied and written history from the time of
Herodotus ('the father of history') onwards. He demonstrates that
until the nineteenth century its relevance, as a means of enabling
men to come to terms with contemporary problems and also as a
means of instruction, was among history's main characteristics.
Lloyd then reviews the emergence of 'scientific' history, in which
considerations of relevance were rejected in favour of establishing
in minute detail 'what happened in the past'. In short, he analyses
the background to what is called in this book 'the professional
approach' to the practice of history. At the same time, he examines
the circumstances in which history became established in our
universities, and shows that this occurred owing specifically to
its presumed relevance as a medium of education.

The second chapter is devoted to a critical analysis of the
professional approach. Connell-Smith demonstrates the false
premises upon which this is based, but shows that it is attractive
to professional historians and explains their antipathy towards

[1] We are aware that significant efforts have been made in recent years by some
such teachers to develop what we would term the educational relevance of history.
But as a prominent college lecturer has declared, 'it is the universities that must
give the lead: only they can provide the fundamental education upon which the
teachers in the Grammar Schools and the lecturers in the colleges and departments
of education can base their work' (D. B. Heater, 'The Teacher Speaks', in J. L.
Henderson (ed.), *Since 1945: Aspects of Contemporary World History* (1966), p. 46).
While Mr. Heater is here referring specifically to contemporary history, we shall
show that his comment is even more pertinent in relation to history in general.

current demands for 'relevance'. He criticises above all the identification of history with 'the past' and the attempt to divorce the past from the present, which are cardinal features of the professional approach. He affirms that the concern of history is with bringing together the past and the present, and thus he indicates the importance of present circumstances and experience in the historian's work. Connell-Smith then demonstrates the unfortunate consequences of the professional approach for the historian's role as a citizen and as a teacher. He points out how the historian's view of himself as essentially a scholar leads him to project the professional approach into his teaching.

In chapter three Connell-Smith sets out to formulate an approach to the practice of history relevant to the present circumstances of the discipline and of the institutions in which it is practised. As an essential preliminary to this formulation he looks at contemporary history, whose attributes have important implications for professional historians. In Connell-Smith's judgement, the hostility often shown by professional historians to the very notion of contemporary history reveals further weaknesses in the professional approach. At the same time it shows an instinctive realisation that what such historians regard as 'real' history is no longer possible under the changed circumstances. But in a contemporary approach – which Connell-Smith advocates – the only real history is that which has contemporary significance, even though it may be concerned with historical phenomena remote from our own time. He shows the importance of a contemporary approach in harmonising the roles of the professional historian as scholar, citizen and teacher.

In the fourth chapter Lloyd shows that there is an urgent need for professional historians to address themselves more seriously to the problems of teaching, and this requires a fundamental alteration of approach to history as an academic discipline. He argues that many university teachers of history adhere to an 'information-orientated' approach to teaching, even though they tend to relegate information to secondary significance in pressing the claims of their discipline as a medium of education. He shows how the amateurishness of historians as educators has extremely important implications in general for their ability to promote their pupils' intellectual development and in particular for the vexed problem of selecting university entrants. Lloyd suggests more effective ways in which history may be taught and examined. He refers to the researches of educational psychologists into ways of developing the mental powers of pupils, and notably to what are called 'convergent' and 'divergent' thinking. He demonstrates the significance of these researches for the teaching of history, and the special qualities of history as a medium of education – if properly taught. Lloyd warns that the present favourable ratio of university teachers to their students is not warranted by the teaching methods widely employed in universities at the present time. While that ratio does make possible the more relevant methods he suggests, a continuation of the present methods positively invites a much less favourable ratio, since information-orientated methods can be applied to much greater numbers of students than at present by the same number of teachers. In teaching, as in historical scholarship, a more relevant approach is needed to prevent the decline of the discipline.

In the conclusion we set side by side the characteristics of the professional approach and of our own, in order to leave no doubt in the reader's mind of the fundamental differences between them. Then we reiterate our reasons for urging that the professional approach be abandoned: both on account of its inherent contradictions and of its irrelevance to our present circumstances. We look at criticisms which have recently been made of the practice of history, and demonstrate how they fall far short of the fundamental alterations of approach for which we call. Finally, we draw attention to the wider implications of our argument in terms of the changing circumstances of historical studies themselves, of the institutions in which they are pursued, and of the society which those institutions exist to serve.

I The Historical Background

In the fifth century B.C. Herodotus of Halicarnassus wrote an account of the Persian wars with the Greeks. He was later described by Cicero, and has since been recognised by convention, as the 'father of history'. This is a comforting convention for historians, as it offers them the assurance that theirs is a venerable discipline. Nowadays, however, many professional historians take the view that 'real' history began as recently as the nineteenth century. Owing particularly to the influence of Ranke, it was then that historical studies became devoted to the aim of establishing what actually happened in the past.[1] For such historians, what was written before Ranke may be evidence and may even be literature. Judged as history, it will not do. Such a view lies at the heart of the 'professional approach', which is described and criticised in the second chapter of this book. My purpose in this chapter is to place that approach in an historical perspective, by reviewing the practice of history in classical Greece and Rome and afterwards in England.

Briefly, I believe that Herodotus did indeed write history and that subsequently history continued to be written, in different ways at different times, although its status was relatively inferior among the disciplines practised by learned men. The aim of philosophers and mathematicians, theologians and natural scientists, was to discover universal truths. By comparison, while those who applied themselves to history sometimes made large claims for their subject, they practised it mainly for its relevance to practical purposes. Amongst such purposes, two were especially prominent. History was repeatedly held to have relevance as a means of enabling men to come to terms with contemporary

[1] Leopold von Ranke (1795–1886), professor of history at Berlin. His famous phrase, expressing his aim of establishing what had happened *wie es eigentlich gewesen*, occurs in the preface to his first major work, the *Histories of the Romance and Germanic Peoples, 1494–1535* (1824).

7

problems. Allied to this was its relevance as a medium of instruction. From such considerations of relevance history derived its strength. They also prompted discerning historians to present their work in a manner comprehensible to laymen and to exploit it as a medium of literature. But in the nineteenth century a number of developments, in philosophy, in science, in education and in history itself, endowed historical studies with a new status and presented historians with a new opportunity. The status derived from what was hoped of history as a human science, capable of yielding conclusions comparable with those to which, hitherto, other disciplines had aspired. Such hopes neither have been, nor are likely to be, justified. Nevertheless, considerations of academic status have prompted historians to set relevance aside and to persist in an approach whereby history is studied 'for its own sake'. This has prevented them from realising the opportunity that was also presented to them in the nineteenth century. For history was then established in a prominent place in university curricula owing specifically to its presumed relevance as a medium of education.

So let us begin with Herodotus. Born in that crucible frontier region of Asia Minor where eastern and western civilisations met, his early interests appear to have lain in matters of geography and ethnology. These interests are apparent in his historical writings, which include much that has seemed to later readers to be digression from his main historical theme. This appearance of digression is heightened by Herodotus's having constructed his work in accordance with elaborate literary conventions which are unfamiliar to later readers accustomed to linear argument and to simple, sequential narrative. In a sense, Herodotus as literary craftsman is too sophisticated for us, though his contemporaries appreciated him well enough. In another sense, Herodotus as historian is too naif. He lacked the means to establish an exact chronology. He lacked the ability to discriminate between trivial and significant causes. Basing his account of the Persian wars upon observations from his own travels and upon what men had told him about events which had occurred in their lifetimes, he exhibited credulity as well as critical sense and a liking for legends as well as for facts. Despite his scientific interests, powerful imagination and gift for captivating the Athenian audiences whom he addressed – sometimes, one suspects, because of these latter qualities – he has often been dismissed as a mere teller of tales.

But however limited his means of attaining it, Herodotus had a serious historical purpose in view. He published his researches, as he declared at the outset,[1]

> in the hope of thereby preserving from decay the remembrance of what men have done, and of preventing the great and wonderful actions of the Greeks and the Barbarians from losing their due meed of glory; and withal to put on record what were their grounds of feud.

In seeking to discover how and why that 'feud' had occurred he did not deal, like a philosopher, in abstractions. Although he employed literary artifices he did not rely, like a poet or an orator, upon imagination, style and the plausible. For Herodotus, explanations for what men had done in any particular situation lay in other actions and other events in which men had demonstrably been engaged and for which men were responsible. Because of this, he wrote history. But he did not write it for its own sake. When he argued the historical importance of decisions taken responsibly by the free choice of courageous men,[2] he was addressing the Greeks of his own day. This was how the Athenians had saved Greece from Persian imperialism. Now the Athenians were threatened as a result of their own imperialism, by decadence from within and by hostility on the part of other Greeks in the Peloponnesian War. In past experience Herodotus found guidance for contending with present circumstances.

Perhaps he marred his work, and obscured its purpose, by too much indulgence in the pleasures of the *raconteur*. Certainly, Herodotus's most notable Greek successor, Thucydides, criticised him for this, and so heralded the interminable debate amongst historians over how they ought to approach their task. In the classical era the argument turned on how far history should be a vehicle for rhetorical writing calculated to excite emotion, or how far historians ought to eschew literary embellishments in the interests of accuracy.[3] Thucydides took the latter view, and was

---

[1] *The History of Herodotus*, I.1, trans. G. Rawlinson (1910), vol. i, p. 1.

[2] For example, VII.139 (ibid., vol. ii, pp. 171–2). For assessments of Herodotus, see M. Finley, *The Greek Historians* (1959), p. 6; M. Grant, *The Ancient Historians* (1970), pp. 35–7; J. L. Myres, *Herodotus, Father of History* (1953), pp. 56–7, 66; J. E. Powell, *The History of Herodotus* (1939), pp. 84–6.

[3] For example, A. H. Lesky, *A History of Greek Literature*, trans. J. Willis and C. de Heer (1966), p. 625.

aware of its implications. Indeed, there is in his approach an attractive realism. 'The absence of romance in my history', he remarked,[1] 'will, I fear, detract somewhat from its interest.' While he affirmed that his account of contemporary military and political history was based 'upon the clearest data', he claimed for his conclusions no more than that they were 'as exact as can be expected in matters of such antiquity'. It was for its relevance that he considered his history worthwhile: if it

> be judged useful by those inquirers who desire an exact knowledge of the past as an aid to the interpretation of the future, which in the course of human things must resemble if it does not reflect it, I shall be content.

Even this was to claim more for history than others would concede. For Socrates, as reported by Plato, true knowledge came through philosophical inquiry, not through contemplating the changing world of human affairs, that 'twilight world of things that come into existence and pass away' which yielded 'only opinions and beliefs which shift to and fro'.[2] For others the place of Clio, daughter of Memory as Herodotus himself had implicitly acknowledged, was firmly among the muses, goddesses of the arts, where history kept company with dancing, flute-playing, comedy. Nevertheless, Herodotus and Thucydides had their serious successors. Argument continued among these later historians of Greece and Rome over the respective claims of accuracy and literary effect. But it was essentially an argument over means rather than ends. Even those who stressed the importance of accuracy had no doubt that simply to establish what had happened in the past would be mere antiquarianism. Historians must undertake more than that. They sought in past events practical illustrations of the hand of providence, practical examples of those human qualities that seemed to them excellent and worth propagating – above all, relevance to current needs. Thus Polybius in particular, as he re-stated the continuing argument, might insist upon the historian's duty 'to record with fidelity what was actually said or done, however commonplace it may be'. But this was because 'the object is to benefit the learner';

---

[1] Quotations from Thucydides are taken from Book I of the *History of the Peloponnesian War*, trans. R. Crawley (1876), pp. 14–15.

[2] *The Republic of Plato*, trans. F. M. Cornford (1941), pp. 214–15.

because 'knowledge of the past is the readiest means men can have of correcting their conduct'; and because 'the study of history is in the truest sense an education, and a training for political life'.[1]

Moreover, for the major historians of Greece and Rome – Xenophon, Caesar, Sallust, Tacitus – political life was no mere matter of academic discussion, but a reality in which they themselves were actively engaged. Each of these suffered vicissitudes in his own political career. Each of them either experienced severe challenges to his own ambitions or witnessed betrayal of the principles he avowed. All of them looked to the past for reassurance and justification. Such inquiry, they thought, was an appropriate occupation for men of affairs: not at all for its own sake, but owing to its relevance to those affairs. It is in Caesar that the connection between recording events and participating in them is most evident; his *Commentaries* were a deliberate exercise in propaganda, intended to counter opposition to him at Rome.[2] But even Tacitus, perhaps the finest of these historians, far less inclined than Caesar to grind a personal axe or than Sallust to salve personal disappointments, wrote as a prominent, conscientious citizen, acutely concerned over the political problems of his day. He believed 'that serious history was a task for the politician':[3] that through its study guidance for present and future conduct could be gained, and the essential Roman virtues reasserted at a time when emperors had abused power and the Empire itself was in danger.

This was the approach of the senatorial tradition in historical writing. Of course, it was the product of historical circumstances. Arguably, if more non-senators or more non-politicians such as Livy had written history, they might have done so in another way. Arguably, too, if these same highly intelligent and cultivated men had had at their disposal the technical resources proudly commanded by modern professionals, they might have approached their studies differently. They might have laid even more stress than they did upon factual accuracy because they could have reposed somewhat greater faith in the possibility of

[1] Quotations from Polybius are taken from II.56 and I.1 of his *Universal History*, as translated by Finley, op. cit., pp. 466 and 442–3.

[2] See, for example, M. Grant, *Julius Caesar* (1969), p. 94.

[3] For assessments of Tacitus, versatile author of the biographical *Agricola* and the ethnographical *Germania* as well as the *Histories* and *Annals* of imperial Rome, see T. A. Dorey (ed.), *Tacitus* (1969), from which (p. 121) the quotation is taken.

arriving at it. If they had had more documents to hand they might have emphasised their importance rather more and that of hearsay testimony and other evidence rather less. If studying past events had been more intrinsically rewarding they might have regarded it more highly as a purely intellectual exercise. But all this is the merest conjecture. The fact is that they wrote what they believed to be history. It is foolish to deny the validity of their belief: as foolish as to overlook the equally plain fact that they wrote history for its relevance to their contemporaries and to themselves.

By comparison with the achievement of the classical era, historical writing in medieval England is undeniably impover-ished, in content and in manner. There was, it would seem, little inclination on the part of distinguished citizens to concentrate attention, when they wrote, upon the activities and qualities of men. Was not the intellectual life of medieval English society dominated by the Church? Was not the Church the agent upon earth of God's will? Men merely fulfilled the universal plan, with no control over His purpose nor over their own destiny. In consequence, simply to record men's activities was an unimportant task to be discharged, if at all, by unimportant clerks. In general their achievement was in keeping with their station. Moreover,

> History was no part of medieval education: no one taught history and no one learnt it. It had no place in the religious life: nor in the activities of the cathedral school: nor later in the universities.[1]

Those universities were dominated by the teachings of Aristotle; and had not Aristotle pronounced history to be less worthy of serious attention than poetry? It was a theocentric enough age for poetry. And as for history, it is a small matter for the followers of Ranke to sweep a thousand years aside as a time when the subject languished.

But medieval England deserves a kinder verdict. Of course, her historical writing was not that of the ancient world; nor was it that of Renaissance humanism, nor of more recent centuries. Yet at Jarrow in 731 Bede completed his *Ecclesiastical History of the English Nation*, addressed specifically to laymen, and recognised by modern authorities as the finest historical work to have

[1] V. H. Galbraith, *Historical Research in Medieval England* (1951), p. 11.

appeared in western Europe from the fall of Rome to the twelfth century.[1] In that century William of Malmesbury produced historical writing which, it has been authoritatively claimed, was the work of 'a scholar who has examined his materials with acumen and presents his synthesis in polished chapters designed for the cultured reader'.[2] And at St. Albans a century later, evidently thinking of himself as an historian (however later scholars may think of his work), Matthew Paris 'kept himself well enough informed of current events in all parts of Europe to write one of the fullest and most elaborate of all medieval chronicles'.[3] Whatever their deficiencies, these activities are not to be ignored. It seems that intellectual circumstances, and especially the circumstances of Norman England,[4] were after all not so unfavourable to the writing of history. What is certain is that none of these historians studied the past for its own sake. The declared intention of the most indiscriminatingly inquisitive of these three, who was also the most intrigued by secular matters, was still more firmly the purpose of the rest:

> to perpetuate notable events in writing, for the praise of God and in order that posterity should be instructed by reading, how to avoid those things which deserve punishment, and how to engage in the good things which are rewarded by God.[5]

It was in this spirit of instruction that members of the religious houses of England made their contribution to historical writing, and thereby left their individual mark upon the changing character of history. In doing so they preserved for posterity much of the heritage of the classical world, together with information regarding their own times. But their object was to expound the will of God; and they practised history essentially for its relevance to that didactic aim.

By the sixteenth century the approach to history was altering once again. In England, as in Europe at large, the age of Renaissance and Reformation, of maritime expansion and domestic

---

[1] See the Preface to Bede's *History*; and J. Campbell, in T. A. Dorey (ed.), *Latin Historians* (1966), p. 160.

[2] R. R. Darlington, quoted in Galbraith, op. cit., p. 16.

[3] R. Vaughan, *Matthew Paris* (1958), pp. 111, 125, 11.

[4] See R. W. Southern, *Medieval Humanism and other Studies* (1970), pp. 51, 60, 160–2.

[5] Quoted in Vaughan, op. cit., p. 151.

political and social change, was characterised by intellectual restlessness, by a tendency to question received dogma. Scepticism and humanism went hand in hand, each nourished by critical interest in antiquity and its intellectual achievement. This interest included a taste for the historians of Greece and Rome. While their popularity varied and fluctuated with time, contemporaries preferred those ancient historians whose experience and attitudes seemed relevant to their own. Thus,

> The rise of absolute monarchs and their courts, the rise in frequency of civil wars and revolutions between 1550 and 1650, are all likely to have made Tacitus more popular because he wrote in similar conditions.[1]

Prominent political figures read him: among them, Elizabeth's rebellious favourite, the Earl of Essex, whose books at Cambridge in 1581 included four volumes of Roman history in addition to Plutarch's works.[2] But not only did literate Englishmen mark the classics. Not only did literate and illiterate alike attend and applaud theatrical representations of past events from the ancient world. As the events of Tudor and Stuart England unfolded, men were increasingly inclined to explore for themselves less distant circumstances: not as avenues of escape from the problems of the present, but for the relevance of those circumstances to their own uncertain and turbulent age.

However disturbed it was a constructive age, of practical achievement by practical men, not least in the realm of institutions. For practical reasons the Defender of the Faith had taken dogged steps to revise the religion of his people. His followers justified their Anglican church by reference not only to theology but to history as well. It was for this purpose that the martyrologist John Foxe compiled his *Acts and Monuments*; Archbishop Matthew Parker, his collection of relevant books and manuscripts. The House of Commons was serving its apprenticeship and winning a political initiative in its relationship with the Crown. Its members vindicated their behaviour by means of strenuous appeals to historical precedent. Change was widespread and far-

---

[1] P. Burke, 'A Survey of the Popularity of Ancient Historians, 1450–1700', *History and Theory*, vol. v (1966), p. 151.

[2] Longleat House, Devereux Papers, vol. v, fo. 54 (I am grateful to the Marquess of Bath for permission to cite from this source).

reaching. The role of the monarch's principal servants was foreshadowing that of modern ministers of state; their subordinates, that of the modern civil service; and local administration was being consolidated by growing numbers of influential magistrates whose competence, though variable, owed at least something to the advice of William Lambarde, himself keenly interested in antiquarian and historical matters.[1] Englishmen were revaluing and reshaping their church, their law, their government; new men, engaged in new departures, were ready, however hesitantly, to overhaul their inheritance and even to abandon portions of it. And as they did so, 'Common lawyers, churchmen, government officials, and Parliament-men all studied the past in order to judge the policies and problems of the present'.

But this entailed more than mere compilation, or piecemeal references to past occurrences. A substantial body of historical writing was produced: writing of such quality and significance as to constitute what one modern authority has termed an 'historical revolution'.[2] In it, God was still recognised as the prime mover of all things. But writers were disposed to concentrate their attention seriously and at length upon men and upon secular affairs. They applied themselves to source-material, approaching it with scepticism and sharpened critical wits. Nevertheless, lacking the arrogance of a later age they knew that they could deal with the past 'but as posterity will with us (which ever thinkes itself the wiser) that will judge likewise of our errors according to the cast of their imaginations'.[3] Knowing this, they self-consciously reflected and aimed to form contemporary preoccupations and contemporary opinion. The history they wrote was patriotic and political. Some, like Ralegh, were actively engaged in affairs; for him, 'historical evidence was the raw material for political judgement, for adjusting institutions to suit changing

[1] Lambarde, author of the *Eirenarcha* which set out the duties of justices of the peace and ran to numerous editions, also made a compilation of early English laws, wrote extensively on the topography and antiquities of Kent, and was Keeper of the Records in the Tower of London.

[2] F. S. Fussner, *The Historical Revolution: English Historical Writing and Thought, 1580–1640* (1962), from which the foregoing quotation is also taken (p. 302). The historical writing of the English Reformation is discussed in F. J. Levy, *Tudor Historical Thought* (1967), pp. 79–123; the effect of the dissolution of the monasteries upon historical studies, in M. McKisack, *Medieval History in the Tudor Age* (1971).

[3] Samuel Daniel, *The First Part of the Historie of England* (1612), p. 3.

circumstances'.[1] But even William Camden, who devoted his life to teaching and to scholarship, elected to write the history of his own time. In it he 'described and explained the events of Elizabeth's reign almost exclusively by referring to the ideas, questions, and issues which occupied the attention of contemporary statesmen'.[2] And contemporary statesmen accorded him their patronage. In short, by what they wrote these men achieved far more than an exhibition of scholarly expertise. They produced historical literature which, owing to its concern with major themes, was widely read, as it was meant to be, by laymen for its relevance to them.

Their achievement reached its culmination in the first half of the seventeenth century. Subsequently in that century historical scholarship continued to develop in the hands of such men as William Dugdale and George Hickes, whose medieval studies bear the hallmarks of technical expertise and intellectual distinction. For them, as for many humanists before them, 'the mainspring of inquiry had been that in the exploration of the past was to [be] found alike the justification of religious belief and the guide to patriotic action'.[3] But neither the humanists nor their successors won for history an established place among academic disciplines. If the humanists attacked Aristotle, it was Descartes who challenged him most severely; and Descartes was dismissive of history. Lacking the rigour of a true science, it was one of 'those simple forms of knowledge which can be acquired without the aid of reasoning'. It was inaccurate: what history records 'is not portrayed as it really is'. Still more damaging, Descartes did not find relevance in history; for 'when one is too curious about things which were practised in past centuries, one is usually very ignorant about those which are practised in our own time'.[4] It

[1] Christopher Hill, *Intellectual Origins of the English Revolution* (1965), p. 199; cf. P. Lefranc, *Sir Walter Ralegh écrivain: l'oeuvre et les idées* (1968), for an assessment of the influence of circumstances and of contemporary attitudes upon Ralegh and his *History of the World*.

[2] Fussner, op. cit., pp. 242–3. On Camden's accuracy as an historian, see H. A. Lloyd, 'Camden, Carmarden and the Customs', *The English Historical Review*, vol. lxxxv (1970), pp. 776–87.

[3] D. C. Douglas, *English Scholars, 1660–1730* (1951), p. 275. Dugdale was perhaps most notably the historian of *Warwickshire* (1656); while Hickes brought comparative philology to bear upon the study of Anglo-Saxon charters.

[4] Quotations from Descartes are taken from *The Search after Truth* and the *Discourse on the Method*, in E. S. Haldane and G. R. T. Ross (trans.), *The Philosophical Works of Descartes*, vol. i (1955), pp. 84–5, 309.

was through philosophy, mathematics and science that learned men hoped to uncover the true nature of things. In such a climate, prospects seemed poor for history in the coming age of reason. Descartes too had his critics: most notably in England, where Locke and Hume emerged as the leading opponents of Cartesian principles. Yet neither took history as seriously as philosophy. Although Hume found it worthwhile to dress his philosophical and political opinions in the trappings of the past, his historical writing was no exhibition of microscopic inquiry into the past for its own sake. Rather, it was in harmony with the view of his fellow-Tory Bolingbroke, who ridiculed pedantic studies which 'may serve to render us mere antiquaries and scholars', and emphasised

> that history is philosophy teaching by examples how to conduct ourselves in all the situations of private and public life; that therefore we must apply ourselves to it in a philosophical spirit and manner; that we must rise from particular to general knowledge, and that we must fit ourselves for the society and business of mankind.[1]

Despite Descartes, such opinions still drew men to practise history, for its practical relevance to contemporary affairs and as a means of instruction. Thus William Robertson, whose best-selling work was intended 'not only for those who are called to conduct the affairs of nations, but for such as inquire and reason concerning them'. His *History of Scotland* was admired by Chesterfield, who judged recent history, in which 'any man of common sense may by common application be sure to excel', a useful training-ground for the diplomatic service.[2]

Others than statesmen found history relevant in various ways. Notwithstanding Bolingbroke's strictures, backwoods gentlemen and clerics were founding societies of antiquaries in the shires of England and omnivorously collecting remains, for the indulgence of private curiosity and the gratification of local pride. Hardly

[1] Henry St. John, Viscount Bolingbroke, *Letters on the Study and Use of History*, vol. i (1752), pp. 57–8. For resemblances between aspects of the thought of Hume and of Bolingbroke, see G. Giarizzo, *David Hume* (1962), pp. 69–70.

[2] Quotations from Robertson are taken from his collected *Works* (1840), vol. iii, p. v; see also J. B. Black, *The Art of History* (1926), p. 128. For Chesterfield's proposal of patronage for Robertson, see *Works*, op. cit., vol. i, p. xxii. The Earl's opinion of history is quoted in C. H. Firth, 'Modern History in Oxford, 1724–1841', *The English Historical Review*, vol. xxxii (1917), p. 2.

more discriminating than theirs were the interests of the members of London's Society of Antiquaries; yet its royal charter of 1751 roundly declared that

> the study of Antiquity, and the History of former times, has ever been esteemed highly commendable and useful, not only to improve the minds of men, but also to incite them to virtuous and noble actions.[1]

And in Gibbon's hands, something akin to the senatorial tradition of historical writing was gloriously revived, in company with – indeed, in subordination to – the classical vein of history as literature. Though he looked back to a golden age when the Antonine Emperors were 'actuated only by the love of order and justice', his own political and religious views were unstable, and he had no great philosophy of history to propagate. Though he read widely and retentively, he never covered himself with dust by labouring through manuscripts – unlike Camden, associate of an earlier society of antiquaries. Cynical at heart, Gibbon set out expressly to win literary fame and found the means in history, 'the most popular species of writing, since it can adapt itself to the highest or the lowest capacity'.[2]

Into the nineteenth century history prospered as literature, its practitioners deliberately addressing themselves to wide audiences. Uninhibited by their awareness of their own involvement with their own time, they, like Burckhardt, approached history as *'on every occasion the record of what one age finds worthy of note in another'.*[3] Measures of worth varied. For Carlyle, reacting romantically against the rationalism of the Enlightenment, it lay in those great men through whose exercise of individual power nations were made great. For Macaulay, it was his country's physical, intellectual and moral progress since the Glorious Revolution of

[1] *A Copy of the Royal Charter and Statutes of the Society of Antiquaries of London* (1800), p. 1.

[2] Quotations from Gibbon are taken from *The Decline and Fall of the Roman Empire*, ed. J. B. Bury, vol. i (1926), p. 9; and from *Memoirs of My Life*, ed. G. A. Bonnard (1966), p. 157.

[3] J. Burckhardt, *Judgements on History and Historians*, trans. H. Zohn (1959), p. 158. The emphasis, indicated by italics, is Burckhardt's own, who continues: 'Every historian will have a special selection, a different criterion for what is worth communicating, according to his nationality, subjectivity, training, and period'.

1688. While he admired Ranke's work, he was no devotee of the past for its own sake. 'No past event', he affirmed,[1]

> has any intrinsic importance. The knowledge of it is valuable only as it leads us to form just calculations with respect to the future. A history which does not serve this purpose, though it may be filled with battles, treaties and commotions, is as useless as the series of turnpike tickets collected by Sir Matthew Mite.

But the influences of rationalism and of Ranke have been far greater upon the practice of history than have those of Carlyle and Macaulay, for all their appeal to their contemporaries. From rationalism sprang the attitude that gave rise to scientific positivism: implicitly as authoritarian a doctrine as anything Carlyle ever wrote, and hugely attractive in an age of scientific advance and scientific excitement. From Ranke has descended a line of professional historians committed to the first part of the positivist programme and dedicated to the accumulation of facts and the study of documents.

The positivist programme began with observation of separate and particular facts existing independently of the observer. For historians, this meant establishing precisely what had happened in the past. The programme would proceed by discerning the principles governing the relations of established facts with each other, their types and their recurrences; and ultimately, these principles would be erected into laws. Positivist philosophers tended to move rather too eagerly and prematurely into the later phases of this operation. Historians were increasingly preoccupied by the first. Thus preoccupied, they concentrated their attention upon the preservation of manuscripts: for was it not in these that the past itself was preserved and the facts enshrined? Moreover, the assistance of the state itself was forthcoming. On the eve of Victoria's reign astonishment was expressed in Parliament at

> the quantity of remains of rats which were found amongst the [Public] Records. On one occasion the skeleton of a cat had been found amongst them. Evidence too appeared, that the Public Records had served a better purpose than rat-traps. The Public Records had been boiled down for glue,

[1] T. B. Macaulay, *Works: Essays and Biographies*, vol. i (1898), pp. 212–13.

and the cleaner and better sort had been converted into jellies by the confectioners.[1]

For thrifty Victorians this would not do. Official steps were taken to remedy that situation. But for scholars, this alone was not enough. If without what was contained in manuscripts there could be no history, that information must be placed as widely as possible at the disposal of historians. Hence the Historical Manuscripts Commission, the *Calendars* of State Papers, the Rolls Series; hence, too, the Royal Historical Society, founded in 1868, its first Literary Director declaring:

> The Society aims at the reproduction and illustration of rare historical tracts, and the recovery, from recondite sources, of materials which might illustrate the less explored paths of national and provincial history.[2]

In this there was little sign of relevance. But in these ways, publications multiplied of transcripts, or at least of extensive *précis*, from those indispensable means to historical knowledge, the past's advertisements of itself to the present: manuscripts.

Since history was concerned with past events, this seemed unexceptionable. Manuscripts had certainly 'happened in the past'. Whether anything more could be said of them remained to be seen. For the time being, the problems of determining precisely what was contained in them became more and more absorbing. Of course, manuscripts had been studied before; and the argument for accuracy in historical studies was an ancient one. But never before had that argument carried so much weight. Thanks to Ranke, scientific exactitude now seemed possible. And thanks to Darwin, it seemed essential. For owing to developments in the natural sciences, history seemed at last to have scientific potential. Its former weakness when measured against other subjects had become its strength. Hitherto men had sought, by means of philosophy and mathematics, theology and natural science, to arrive at knowledge of the nature of things which they conceived of as immutable. History's concern was with the changing world of human affairs, the flux that intervened between men and truth, the 'twilight world' of Socrates. As such, it had

---

[1] *Hansard's Parliamentary Debates*, series iii, vol. xxxi (1836), col. 556. In a sense, depredations by rats are necessary to the professional approach: see below, p. 36.

[2] Preface to vol. i of the *Transactions of the Royal Historical Society* (1872); cf. the charter of the London Society of Antiquaries, quoted above, p. 18.

had no place among the branches of higher learning. But now, evolutionary theory proclaimed that all things were continually in process of change. Approaches in the natural sciences were transformed; and to history fell the task of demonstrating scientifically how the affairs and institutions of civilised man had changed through time.

So, like Niebuhr, more and more technicians in the historical laboratory laboured to 'dissect words as an anatomist dissects bodies'.[1] But unlike him, many of them aspired to nothing more creative. The narrowness of some proposals aroused concern even in their official sponsors. When the Master of the Rolls advocated that in chronicles and documents printed in the Series there should be very little editorial comment beyond 'what might be necessary to establish the correctness of the text', the Treasury Lords mildly suggested the advantages of including at least 'a biographical account of the author . . . and an estimate of his historical credibility and value'.[2] Moreover, the immediate effect of studying manuscripts was to sharpen disagreement upon historical matters. Earlier Macaulay had ridiculed Edward Nares[3] for his unreadable study of Lord Burghley, monstrous with erudition and irrelevance. Now exchanges between historians became more acrimonious. Although Stubbs and Freeman might butter one another, Freeman had only acid to pour on Froude despite the latter's lavish citations of manuscript sources in his work.[4] Narrow correctness and learned controversy were ominous signs – as we shall see. But in the middle of the nine-

[1] Quoted in G. P. Gooch, *History and Historians in the Nineteenth Century* (1928), p. 19. The Dane, B. G. Niebuhr, worked in Germany; his influence, like those of Ranke, the Göttingen historians and other Germans, has been formative upon modern historical studies – as, in their early stages, was French influence. Significantly, English historians tend to look askance at recent developments in French historical studies; cf. below, p. 31.

[2] See the prefatory notice, dated December 1857, to the volumes of the Rolls Series.

[3] Formally appointed Regius Professor of Modern History at Oxford in 1814; see below, p. 25. Cf. the merits found by Macaulay in Ranke's *History of the Popes* (1834–6): 'the work of a mind fitted both for minute researches and *for large speculations*' (*Critical and Historical Essays contributed to the Edinburgh Review* (1850), pp. 217, 535; my italics). In many ways, Ranke has been poorly understood and poorly served by his professed disciples; cf. below, p. 112, note 1.

[4] All three held Oxford's regius chair, J. A. Froude succeeding the younger Edward Freeman despite the latter's ferocious attacks upon him in the *Saturday Review* for 'utter carelessness as to facts and utter incapacity to distinguish right from wrong'. By contrast, Freeman regarded William Stubbs as his master; the allusion is to a satirical verse of the time.

teenth century, as the official series of document publications got under way, there occurred a development of fundamental importance to English historical studies. History won a recognised place in the curricula of English universities.

Yet it is not the rise of scientific history that explains this development. Rather, it is the relevance found by contemporaries in history as a medium of education. We have already seen that such a quality was prominent amongst those found in history by men who, in the classical era and subsequently in England, had approached it in their different ways at different times. Early in the seventeenth century, and again in the eighteenth, there were attempts to establish the subject in the universities. These were comparatively unsuccessful, largely owing to the character of the universities themselves. In the nineteenth century that character was changing under the influence of men who held conflicting views of the aims of education and of the role of universities in society. It was in these peculiar circumstances that history emerged as a subject capable of reconciling and of furthering these aims. In order to show this, I will briefly describe the changing character of English universities and their connection with history, concluding with an assessment of the way in which the subject became established there.

During the institutional changes of the sixteenth century the universities had not escaped scrutiny. For their reliance upon Aristotelian logic as adapted by the schoolmen, they were severely criticised. Formerly, modes of instruction geared to those procedures would seem to have been appropriate enough. When printed books were not available and handwritten ones expensive, teaching and learning had principally to be conducted by means of oral exchanges between teachers and pupils. For the sake of orderliness and coherence, set rules were essential. Similar considerations dictated the cardinal emphasis upon memory, the art of orderly recollection, practised so that the mind might retain information otherwise not easily available. Further, for most young students the medieval universities were 'simply the door to the Church; and the door to the Church at that time meant the door to professional life'.[1] They existed in order to

---

[1] H. Rashdall, *The Universities of Europe in the Middle Ages*, new edn. (1936), vol. iii, p. 445. I do not, of course, mean to imply that there had been no criticism and no change in universities in the medieval period.

train clerics who would staff the institutions of church and state. They had done so well enough by these methods. But now the institutions and their personnel were changing. Laymen were entering the universities in ever-increasing numbers. Many were dissatisfied with what they found there. Disenchanted, like Marlowe's Faustus, with logic for its own sake, they sought areas of study which offered a greater degree of practical relevance. Such was the attitude in Paris of Peter Ramus, who had outraged conservative opinion with his thesis that Aristotle had been wrong in everything. His views spread to England. Among those who helped to spread them was Fulke Greville. Acting on the basis of such views, Greville attempted in 1627 to found at Cambridge 'a Publique Lecture of Historie'.[1]

Greville's purpose, evident in the qualifications he laid down for eligibility to hold his Readership, was to provide a counter-balance to ecclesiastical influence and a measure of useful instruction by practical men. 'None shalbe eligible that is in holie Orders', he ruled,

> because this Realme affordeth manie preferements for divines, fewe or none for Professors of humane learning, the use and application whereof to the practise of life is the maine end, and scope of this foundation ... Such as have travelled beyond the seas, and soe have added to their learning, knowledge of the moderne languages, and experience in forraigne parts; and likewise such as have been brought upp, and exercised in publique affaires, shalbe accounted most eligible.

Such a man was found in a graduate of Leyden University, who came to Cambridge and began to lecture. But not for long. Archbishop William Laud was given to understand that the lecturer's remarks contained a dangerous relevance to the English political situation, for he seemed to maintain on historical grounds that kings ruled by popular consent. The lectures were prohibited. At Oxford five years previously William Camden, who had also enjoyed Greville's patronage, had likewise attempted to found a Readership in history. Like Greville he preferred 'a man who,

---

[1] J. B. Mullinger, *The University of Cambridge*, vol. iii (1911), pp. 674-7; p. 676 for the quotation that follows. Fulke Greville, Baron Brooke, was a poet, patron of letters and minor political figure. Ramus maintained his thesis for his Master's degree, at the age of twenty-one. For his educational approach, see below, p. 97.

besides his abilities of learning sufficient for such a place, is known
to be of good experience, (having sometimes travelled)'.[1] He too
had insisted that his Reader 'should read a civil history', making
'such observations, as might be most useful and profitable for the
younger students of the university'.[2] The Oxford authorities
considered ecclesiastical history a more suitable field; and much
contention ensued. In 1636 Laud, as Chancellor of the University,
ruled that the proper subject for those lectures was 'historians of
ancient date and repute'. In the same year the University submitted
to the Laudian statutes, which stressed the prime importance
of Aristotle for its curriculum, and which remained the
effective basis of Oxford government for the next two hundred
years.

It is quite clear that although Camden had had no intention of
provoking controversy neither he nor Greville was concerned
simply to launch historical studies for their own sake. In an age of
growing secularism they had attempted a modest secularisation of
curricula that seemed to them too ecclesiastically orientated. In
effect they had failed. History did continue to be taught by some
tutors at both Oxford and Cambridge, as did other subjects which
had no recognised place in their statutory curricula. But the
statutes prevailed, and the statutes determined that as the century
wore on and England evolved her increasingly commercial
civilisation the universities should set their faces against it.[3] In
the eighteenth century Oxford and Cambridge experienced a
period of decline. They merely provided degrees for parsons and
a veneer of polite learning for gentlemen. This provision was
considered 'primitive' by one of those gentlemen, and 'adapted
to the education of priests and monks'.[4] Perhaps the verdict is
harsh; certainly, in that period the universities harboured some
formidable scholars. Moreover, it is arguable that England's
aristocratic élite required the universities to play in terms of
education no more substantial a role than that of finishing-schools.
But at least one important aristocratic statesman and one distinguished ecclesiastic thought otherwise. In 1724 Secretary of State
Townshend and Bishop Edmund Gibson made the second of the

[1] H. Stuart Jones, 'The Foundation and History of the Camden Chair', *Oxoniensia*,
vol. viii–ix (1943–4), p. 173.

[2] M. H. Curtis, *Oxford and Cambridge in Transition, 1558–1642* (1959), p. 117.

[3] Cf. H. F. Kearney, *Scholars and Gentlemen* (1970), p. 171.

[4] Edward Gibbon, *Memoirs of My Life*, op. cit., p. 49.

two principal attempts to which I have referred to establish history there.

They persuaded King George that Oxford and Cambridge ought to do rather more by way of 'sending forth constant supplies of able and learned men to serve the public both in church and state'.[1] And their advice went beyond general propositions. They proposed specifically that in each university there should be founded a regius professorship in modern history, with responsibility for appointing assistants to teach modern languages. This was done. Undoubtedly the government had political interests at heart as well as public service. Institutions which had received patronage at its hands were likely to feel more kindly disposed towards the Hanoverian dynasty. Whatever its sponsors' motives, they judged history relevant to practical purposes. The regius professorships have prospered in our time. But in the decades following their foundation, characteristic Oxbridge inertia reduced them to the level of sinecures. A young French visitor to Cambridge in 1784 recorded of his escort there that 'Although he is a Professor in one of the colleges he does not know how the teaching is conducted'.[2] The man so rebuked was John Symonds, in fact the first of these regius professors to deliver a regular course of lectures. At Oxford none of them exhibited zeal comparable even with his until the appointment in 1814 of Edward Nares, the object of Macaulay's ridicule. His early diligence was not sustained. But he attributed his disenchantment less to general attitudes than to a fresh circumstance. According to Nares, his failure to command an audience amongst undergraduates derived from their being 'too much occupied in preparing for their public examinations'.

By the early-nineteenth century both universities, aware at last of the need to re-order their affairs, had attempted to do so by retrieving the traditional oral exercises for degrees from the pit of inadequacy and irrelevance into which they had fallen.[3] In the closing decades of the eighteenth century examinations at the Cambridge Senate House had become more rigorous. In 1800

[1] Quoted from the king's letter to the universities, in C. H. Firth, op. cit., p. 5.
[2] D. A. Winstanley, *Unreformed Cambridge* (1935), p. 41.
[3] They were 'nothing but a formal repetition of threadbare questions and answers, transmitted in manuscript from man to man, and admitted unblushingly by the Masters of the Schools' (C. E. Mallet, *A History of the University of Oxford*, vol. iii (1927), p. 165). Masters nowadays blush no more readily; cf. below, pp. 99 ff.

Congregation at Oxford assented to a new statute which enacted that every candidate for a degree be publicly examined by examiners appointed by the University. But greater efforts on the part of some teachers, and greater attention to examining, were not enough to enable the universities to escape censure in the age of reform. Growing concern was expressed both within them and outside at the narrowness of their curricula, the abuses of closed scholarships and fellowships, the imperviousness of colleges to efforts at co-ordinating their activities under a more effective form of university control. In 1850 a royal commission was set up to inquire into their alleged shortcomings. It had an important bearing upon the establishment of history.

University reform is one element in that complex of measures through which the governing class of England in the nineteenth century attempted to reconcile conscience with utility in the management of the nation's common affairs. The list of measures by the government itself which were geared to this attitude is familiar enough: the three major acts that extended the franchise; factory legislation, abolition of religious tests, reform of police, criminal law, trade tariffs. With public utility particularly in mind, central government was also taking a closer look at those bodies and individuals who functioned on its behalf. Municipal and county administration were reformed. In 1854 the Northcote-Trevelyan Report recommended that a central board be established to conduct examinations for all candidates for the civil service. The examinations subsequently introduced included papers in modern history. To return to the University Commissioners, comparable considerations of public utility undoubtedly underpinned that section of their report which stressed the need for more honours schools. Among those it recommended was a school of jurisprudence, political economy and history: subjects considered well-suited to equip students for professional and public life. In consequence, a school of law and modern history was established at Oxford. In 1872 history attained separate status. In the next year a separate History Tripos was created at Cambridge.

But, as distinct from utilitarian considerations, the governing class of Victorian England also adhered to another belief: in improvement of the individual and his capacity to improve himself. The measures adopted on the former grounds to reform the universities did not meet with universal approbation. Already concern had been expressed that owing to the rise of examinations and the rise of careerism the student was being 'sacrificed to a professional or special education of the narrowest kind, stunted in mind, old before his time'.[1] Prominent among those who resisted the rise of both was the celebrated rector of Lincoln College, Mark Pattison. By no means opposed to every kind of reform, prepared indeed to put forward reforming proposals of his own, Pattison nonetheless bemoaned changes which meant that the 'number of those who seek *education* by means of the University is very small compared with the number of those who seek the degree and the social status it confers'.[2] For him and those who, like him, rebelled against attempts to convert the universities into forcing-houses for administrators and diplomats, the aim of a university education ought to be to stimulate and liberate the powers of the individual mind. The establishment of history in English universities owes quite as much to the convictions of such men as these as it does to those whose direct concern was with public utility. In 1854 a chair of history was founded at Owens College, Manchester. Its first incumbent, R. C. Christie,[3] was a disciple of Mark Pattison's. He was succeeded in that chair by A. W. Ward,[4] who in 1872 set out the benefits, as he saw them, of rigorous historical study by undergraduates. Properly conducted, the study of history should provide 'something far beyond the accumulation, and exhibition under examination, of a certain amount of knowledge'. It should equip the student with a

> special kind of power . . . the power of applying to the original treatment of Historical questions Historical knowledge which has been accumulated by reading, which has been sifted by criticism, which has been illustrated by comparison, and which has been invested with a literary form by composition.[5]

[1] Quoted in J. W. Adamson, *English Education, 1789–1902* (1930), p. 80.
[2] Quoted in J. Sparrow, *Mark Pattison and the Idea of a University* (1967), pp. 118–19.
[3] Christie was appointed to the chair in question at the age of twenty-four; a few months later, to the chair of political economy and commercial science; and shortly after that, to the chair of jurisprudence.
[4] Ward was appointed to the chair of English at Owens College in 1866, and became vice-chancellor of the Victoria University of Manchester in 1886.
[5] Quoted in J. O. McLachlan, 'The Origin and early development of the Cambridge Historical Tripos', *Cambridge Historical Journal*, vol. ix (1947–9), pp. 82–3.

In their emphasis upon mental power, Ward's words are strongly reminiscent of Pattison's views regarding the proper purpose of a university education.

These, then, were the peculiar circumstances in which history won its place in the universities. It did so neither for its own sake nor for its scientific potential, but for what men judged to be its relevance to attaining two apparently conflicting aims: on the one hand, public utility; on the other, improvement of individual mental powers. The apparent conflict between these aims has historically been a source of discord and disagreement among persons concerned with education. But it seemed in the nineteenth century that through employing history itself as a medium of education they might after all prove compatible.[1] A view of their potential compatibility by these means is evident in the case for the study of history put by one of Oxford's greatest holders of the regius chair. Celebrated for the range and precision of his own historical scholarship, William Stubbs averred that in its pursuit

> The stock of information accumulated is only secondary in importance to the habits of judgment formed by the study of it. For we want to train not merely students but citizens; and citizens of the great communities – the church and the civilised world; to be fitted not for criticism or for authority in matters of memory, but for action.[2]

Habits of judgement and capacity for action; aptitudes beyond those of merely receiving information and applying stereotyped rules of argument: these were the qualities which its several advocates, on the different occasions we have reviewed, believed that the study of history would cultivate in university students. What they emphasised was not advantages that might be derived from an exact knowledge of past events (the possibility of acquiring which in any case had yet – *and has still* – to be shown). And in the nineteenth century history gained institutional status, owing above all to the relevance it was believed to possess as a medium of education.

---

[1] Cf. the successive chairs held by Christie, above, p. 27, note 3; and, for discussion of discordant approaches in education, below, chapter 4.

[2] 'Inaugural' (7 February 1867), in *Seventeen Lectures on the Study of Medieval and Modern History* (1887), p. 21.

A hundred years have elapsed since history became established in
English universities. During that time there has been a great deal
of historical writing. There has also been a great increase in the
size and number of universities, and a corresponding growth in
the number of professional historians. In Great Britain in 1970
there were 46 universities, 33 of which contained separate departments of history employing a total of 882 historians.[1] If one adds
to these the considerable numbers of ancient, economic, literary
and other historians employed in other departments, it is plain
that historians constitute a significant proportion of the teaching
and research staff in university faculties.[2] From numbers alone it
would seem that history has flourished, and continues to flourish,
as an academic discipline. History would also appear to have
demonstrated its relevance in terms of producing useful citizens.
For entry into the administrative class of the civil service, 'Within
the Arts field, history provides the greatest number of successful
candidates. In 1965, 45 per cent. of all successful candidates had
read history.'[3] Three of the thirteen British prime ministers who
have held office since 1914 were history graduates: a larger
proportion than that yielded by any other single subject.

But none of this affords any guarantee that history will continue to flourish. Much of it testifies only to the facility with
which established members of institutional structures multiply
as the institutions themselves expand. It was within educational
and administrative institutions, and owing specifically to its
presumed relevance as a medium of education, that history won its
place in the nineteenth century. While these institutions have
greatly expanded, they are at present undergoing critical scrutiny
in terms of their relevance to society's needs. But hitherto
sheltered within them, historians have ceased to practise their
discipline with relevance in mind. Heirs to scientific history, they
jealously cultivate the status of practising a major academic

[1] Source: *Commonwealth Universities Yearbook* (1970). This figure includes only
established members of the teaching staffs in designated departments of history,
modern history, or medieval and modern history.
[2] The total number of full-time teaching and research staff in the arts faculties
of British universities in 1968 was 5,255, or 16·7% of the total in all faculties
(Source: University Grants Committee (Department of Education and Science
Series), *Statistics of Education, 1968, vol. 6: Universities* (1970), Table 38).
[3] *The Civil Service, vol. 4: Factual, Statistical and Explanatory Papers; Evidence
submitted to the Committee under the Chairmanship of Lord Fulton, 1966–68* (1968),
p. 334.

discipline. For them, pursuers at last of true learning, research is what matters; and mundane considerations of relevance are a distraction.

Yet they have failed to justify belief in their subject's scientific potential. In other academic fields, great developments have taken place since the mid-nineteenth century. As I have argued, approaches to history were at that time influenced by scientific positivism. In my judgement, the influence of *evolving* positivism, broadly interpreted, has been formative upon the social sciences, upon linguistics, upon philosophy, upon the natural sciences. Discerning relations between separate elements, and defining those relations, is the essence of modern structuralism: an approach which, in recent decades, has been applied with important results over a very wide range of academic fields, and which stems from a view of human experience as a totality. But by contrast, the approach of many professional historians has remained at a rudimentary level of first-stage positivism. Far from considering human experience as a totality, they insist instead upon the autonomy of their particular discipline and particularise further within it. For them, Ranke's endeavour to establish what happened in the past has meant, what happened in minute detail. The details have multiplied; the prospect of scientific explanation has receded. As scientists have observed, 'scientific history' left a 'gap of historical interpretation which the serious historians failed to fill'; and there still continues, crippling in its effects, 'an uncertainty among historians about the *kinds* of explanation which they can legitimately give'.[1] So they cling to a view of history 'for its own sake' and study it – as they believe – accordingly.

Their approach has sustained numerous attacks in the course of the twentieth century. Such attacks have occasionally been made by practising historians. They have largely been conducted, however, in philosophical terms. Reasoned criticisms of historians' preoccupation with attempting to establish, in objective terms, precisely what happened in the past, have also been frequently made by philosophers. British historians have for the most part

[1] J. D. Bernal, *Science in History*, vol. iv: *The Social Sciences: Conclusion* (paperback edn., 1969), p. 1081; S. Toulmin and J. Goodfield, *The Discovery of Time* (paperback edn., 1967), p. 297. While I reject Professor Bernal's view that the only solution for historians lies in a Marxist approach (op. cit., p. 1208), that view in itself constitutes a warning to historians of the outcome of their abandoning to others the task of interpreting historical material in relevant terms. Cf. below, p. 82.

remained unmoved by their arguments. On the continent of Europe (most notably in France) and also in the United States of America, twentieth-century developments in approaches in other academic disciplines – and, more specifically, the rise of structuralism – have won a number of prominent converts from the ranks of professional historians. Again, these developments have had little effect upon the approach of professionals in this country. To press the special merits of any such development is no part of our argument in this book. Nor do we argue for new methods and new techniques. It remains to be seen whether adoption of their neighbours' methodologies and approaches will enable historians to arrive at definitive explanations in terms of general principles for the chains of events which they describe and to which they add through their voluminous researches. At present, there is little indication of it. Even so, the attitude of those who remain conservative in their approach to their discipline and insistent upon autonomy in its practice is all the more disturbing in view of their dismissal of relevance.

I have argued in this chapter that for over two thousand years since Herodotus men continued to practise history, for its contemporary relevance, as a means of instruction, and also as a literary medium. Moreover, this was especially so at two extremely important stages in the history of historical practice in England: the 'historical revolution' of the sixteenth and early-seventeenth centuries; the institutionalising of history in the mid-nineteenth century. At both those times English institutions were undergoing far-reaching change. At the present time English institutions are once more the subject of radical revaluation. In view of the failure of their scientific pretensions, it would seem appropriate for historians to attempt to rediscover and to reaffirm the relevance of their subject. That they have apparently felt little need to do so during the last century is a mark of the sheltered security they have enjoyed within educational institutions. That the need is now urgent is indicated by the pace of mid twentieth-century institutional, social and intellectual change.

It may perhaps be understandable that many historians have failed to respond either to changes in other academic fields or to criticisms of their approach by such outsiders as philosophers. Outsiders by definition cannot know 'real' history from within. Less understandable, however, is their failure to recognise the implications of their own approach. This 'professional approach' is described in the next chapter. In it, there is no attempt to revive philosophical or comparative arguments, such as have been largely ineffectual upon the practice of history in this country. The discussion conducted by Connell-Smith focuses upon how in practice professional historians go about their business. It evaluates this professional approach in terms of a practical situation: contemporary society, of which the historian inescapably forms a part.

2 The Professional Approach

IN the first chapter, Lloyd put the present approach of professional historians to their subject into historical perspective. He demonstrated that, although history has been written and read for many centuries, the approach of present-day historians has evolved only over the last century, and is the product of an identifiable set of historical circumstances. Before the nineteenth century, men studied history in the belief that it possessed relevance to two immediate and practical purposes. First, it was thought that the subject had much to contribute to an understanding of contemporary problems, and particularly political ones. Thus a very great deal of history written prior to the nineteenth century was either contemporary history as such or stemmed directly from a concern with contemporary issues. Studies of this kind might lead the historian to delve into the remote past, but they did not lead him to try to abandon the present – rather the reverse. Secondly, and arising from this awareness of history's contemporary relevance, the subject was thought to possess relevance as a medium of education and instruction.

Lloyd then proceeded to show how this traditional view of history was transformed in the nineteenth century with the emergence of a 'scientific' approach. Under the influence of intellectual developments of that period, notably positivism, historians sought to emulate the scientists in their dispassionate and minute analysis of evidence. They convinced themselves of the possibility of establishing precisely what had happened in the past through the objective and microscopic examination of surviving historical documents, their main source of evidence. Objectivity could be achieved by eliminating the present circumstances of the historian from his consideration of the evidence. Accuracy required the development of specialised techniques. Contemporary relevance was rejected in favour of the 'autonomy' of the subject, which was to be studied 'for its own sake'. By these means historians sought to secure for historical studies status as a major academic discipline.

Just at this time, as Lloyd showed, history acquired a prominent place in our universities. But it did so on the basis of its presumed relevance as a medium of education. Here we have the origins of a contradiction between history as an academic discipline and as a medium of education. The contradiction is not inherent in the subject, but is a consequence of what I have called 'the professional approach' to history. This approach is one which has exalted the status of history as a scholarly discipline to the neglect – and even detriment – of its effectiveness as a medium of education. For professional historians have seen themselves primarily as scholars rather than as educators. Their approach has been encouraged by a view of universities as centres of scholarship rather than as institutions forming part of an educational system. Sheltered within universities so regarded, historians have for long been able to practise their discipline with scant regard for the relevance of their activities to anyone but themselves.

But we live today in circumstances very different from those in which the professional approach emerged in the last century. The universities are undergoing critical scrutiny in terms of their relevance to society's needs. Within them – and in our schools – new disciplines have grown up to challenge history, often claiming greater relevance to broad educational objectives. In this situation I believe the professional approach to be untenable. In my judgement it has long since failed to accomplish its own objectives (themselves misguided) and has led to history's losing its way as an academic discipline. It has allowed history to become ineffective as a medium of education and has greatly diminished its attraction for educated laymen. I shall affirm in this chapter that professional historians will have to formulate a new approach to their subject, re-establishing relevance in a central place among its characteristics and emphasising, as its basic purpose, education and instruction in a rapidly changing society.

Let us begin with a critical analysis of the professional approach. I am not, of course, asserting that all historians subscribe to all the ideas and attitudes which this approach embodies. But all historians – including Lloyd and myself – are importantly influenced by the professional approach, if only because it has so largely shaped the academic environment in which we practise our discipline.

In the professional approach, the historian identifies history with 'the past' which, he affirms, has an objective existence independently of him and his present circumstances. He conceives it to be his purpose to establish accurate knowledge about that past. To achieve it he must deliberately abandon the present, and study the past 'for its own sake' and 'on its own terms'. This will enable him to understand the past 'from within'; to see its problems as the people involved saw them, and to analyse them accordingly. These fundamental aspects of the professional approach are forcefully expressed by Geoffrey Elton, Professor of English Constitutional History at Cambridge, whose book *The Practice of History* has been described as 'the most eloquent statement' of what 'might well be termed the up-to-date hard-line professional position'.[1] Elton, for whom historians are 'necessarily practitioners of the past',[2] has declared:

> The task of history is to understand the past, and if the past is to be understood it must be given full respect in its own right. And unless it is properly understood, any use of it in the present must be suspect and can be dangerous.

Therefore, fashioning a sound instrument for this task 'involves, above all, the deliberate abandonment of the present'.[3] Another Cambridge historian once went so far as to assert that 'The study of the past with one eye, so to speak, upon the present is the source of all sins and sophistries in history'.[4] Here we have, clearly affirmed, that attempt to divorce the past from the present which is central to the professional approach to history.

If professional historians are 'practitioners of the past', they are not general practitioners; they are specialists. They concentrate upon particular historical events and situations, which amount to no more than minute fragments of 'the past'. The explanation of this is pre-eminently of a practical kind. In order to study 'the past' the professional historian has to rely upon the evidence that has survived into the present. For him, this means, above all,

[1] A. Marwick, *The Nature of History* (1970), p. 186.
[2] *The Future of the Past* (1968), p. 6.
[3] *The Practice of History* (paperback edn., 1969), p. 66.
[4] H. Butterfield, *The Whig Interpretation of History* (1931), p. 31. Professor Butterfield later was very considerably to modify this view. See below, p. 42.

documents. In documents he finds, or thinks he finds, the 'facts' of 'the past': actually, of course, a version of some portion of the past to which the documents relate. Obviously, nothing approaching the necessary number of documents has survived for establishing everything that has happened to man in the past. But more than enough documents have survived to keep historians occupied in analysing particular historical events and situations for an indefinite period. Since this is what they actually do, the overall paucity of documents does not present a problem for professional historians, even though they very often lack particular ones. Indeed, the professional approach predicates limited documentation – floods and fire, rats and rot have been aptly described as the historian's great allies[1] – and the now overwhelming mass of material available for historical research presents him with a serious dilemma as I shall show in due course.

The study of many historical documents requires technical expertise. The historian, therefore, has to acquire certain professional skills – diplomatic, palaeographic, linguistic – in order to make an exact analysis of the evidence before him. This is particularly so in the case of medieval history. The employment of technical expertise has been an important factor, for professional historians, in establishing the autonomy of their subject and thus its status as an academic discipline. Historical scholarship has been closely identified with it. Hence medieval history traditionally has been held to be more 'scholarly' than modern history. Moreover, being more remote in time,[2] it appears more easily detachable from the present circumstances of the historian. There can be no doubt that the tradition of textual scholarship associated with medieval history has powerfully influenced the development of the professional approach.

Thus professional historians, theoretically concerned with 'the past', in practice have developed an approach involving the application of technical expertise to documents relating to particular historical situations and events. The study of history for its own sake has become, for individual historians, the study of small fragments from the past for *their* own sake. Historians specialise and have developed specialised skills. Historical

---

[1] David Thomson, *The Aims of History: Values of the Historical Attitude* (1969), p. 19.

[2] Though not necessarily of less contemporary significance. See below, p. 73.

scholarship has come to be identified with the exercise of these skills, and the career of the professional historian to be advanced by his success in this regard. The learned article or monograph addressed to fellow professionals has become the badge of historical learning and the key to advancement in the profession. By comparison with the expertise deployed, the subject matter of these articles and monographs is deemed to be of secondary importance. Most ominous of all, this detailed work on fragments from the past has come to be regarded as 'real' history. Thus has history become professionalised. If Clio is a Muse – and professional historians are fond of referring to 'her' – then they have cast themselves in the role of her high priests.[1] The historian's audience consists no longer of educated laymen, but of fellow professionals. Indeed, with increasing specialisation he is able to communicate meaningfully with only a few of *them*. This, then, is where the professional approach has led us since the advent of scientific history in the last century and history's achievement of status as an academic discipline in our universities.

How is such an approach justified? There are two main lines of argument, both inherent in the development of scientific history under circumstances analysed by Lloyd in the previous chapter. Nineteenth-century historians 'scored so many successes in disposing of lies or legends by the confrontation of crucial facts that they came to think of facts as the indestructible atoms by the adding of which together true history could be composed'.[2] Thus, however small the contributions of individual historians may be in themselves, they add to the sum of our knowledge of the whole. It was openly avowed that such labours would make possible a definitive, universal history in some remote future. At the beginning of this century, for example, in his Inaugural Lecture significantly entitled 'The Science of History', the then Regius Professor of Modern History at Cambridge asserted:

The gathering of materials bearing upon minute local events, the collation of MSS. and the registry of their small variations, the patient drudgery in archives of states and municipalities, all the microscopic research that is carried on by armies of toiling students – it may seem like the bearing of

[1] It is noteworthy that Ranke did speak of historians as priests.
[2] Professor Sir George Clark, in his general introduction to *The New Cambridge Modern History*, vol. i (1957), p. xxiv.

mortar and bricks to the site of a building which has hardly been begun, of whose plan the labourers know but little. This work, the hewing of wood and the drawing of water, has to be done in faith – in the faith that a complete assemblage of the smallest facts of human history will tell in the end. The labour is performed for posterity – for remote posterity . . .[1]

More than a generation later it was asserted, more specifically, that:

Nowadays we think of monographs on various subjects as ideally forming parts of a universal history, so that if their subjects are carefully chosen and their scale and treatment carefully controlled they might serve as chapters in a single historical work . . .[2]

But, again, this was for the future.

Meanwhile, there is a second line of argument, independent of the first though linked with it as a facet of scientific history. This argument, in effect, relieves the historian of responsibility for the consequences of his approach. History as a science involves microscopic analysis; thus it can be regarded as the knowledge of individual facts about the past. Of course science also involves the establishment of general laws; but – as Lloyd indicated[3] – professional historians did not proceed to this, second stage of positivism, and came to regard it as sufficient to discover and state the facts themselves. If one accepts the objective existence of the past, the facts about the past may be thought of as independent of the historian. The latter's role is limited to that of establishing what those facts are. This he does through the use of scientific techniques and the exercise of his expertise. Beyond that, in Professor Elton's words, 'The facts known about the past are in control'[4]; indeed, that a past 'event can be known' is 'all that is required to make it a "fact of history".'[5] Thus, the objective existence of the past and the independence of the facts eliminate the subjective element of the historian's judgement. The facts, in short, dictate the kind of history historians write.

[1] H. Temperley (ed.), *Selected Essays of J. B. Bury* (1930), pp. 16–17.
[2] R. G. Collingwood, *The Idea of History* (1946), p. 27.
[3] See above, p. 30.
[4] *The Practice of History*, op. cit., p. 50.
[5] Ibid., p. 76.

Neither of these arguments in justification of the professional approach to the practice of history is valid. The possibility of writing a universal definitive history is no longer avowed. It cannot even be given serious consideration. In his Inaugural Lecture as Regius Professor of Modern History at Oxford in 1957, Hugh Trevor-Roper declared fancifully (to make a far from fanciful point):

> Armies of research students, organized by a general staff of professors, may in time have mapped out the entire history of the world. We may know, or be able to know, what every unimportant minor official in a government office did every hour of his day, what every peasant paid for his plot in a long extinct village, how every backbencher voted on a private bill in an eighteenth-century parliament.[1]

Trevor-Roper pokes fun at the notion that we should want to possess the kinds of information he mentions, and thus at the absurdity of professional historians being engaged – as so many are – upon just such enterprises as he describes. But he knows very well that the task of mastering more than a fraction of the knowable past is far beyond the capability of the largest conceivable 'armies of research students' as it was already beyond that of the 'armies of toiling students' conjured up by that other regius professor over half a century earlier.[2] As for universal history being constructed from learned monographs, the volumes of so modest a collaborative enterprise as *The New Cambridge Modern History* should dispel any illusions in that regard. In the matter of universal history, historians are in truth for ever travelling hopefully in the confident expectation of never reaching their destination. Bolder spirits who leave their specialised sector to work on the whole process of history can expect short shrift from their fellows,[3] amongst whom in practice (as we have seen) detailed specialisation has become an end in itself: 'real' history.

But what these professional historians are doing, we are told, is dictated by the facts of the knowable past: the second of the two lines of argument justifying the professional approach. This,

[1] *History: Professional and Lay* (1957), pp. 15–16.
[2] See above, p. 37.
[3] One does not have to agree with the interpretations of civilisation put forward by such writers as Spengler and Toynbee to be struck by the hostility with which their syntheses have been greeted by professional historians.

too, cannot survive serious examination. History is written – can only be written – on terms decided by historians. Professor Elton, as we have seen, strongly argues otherwise. Yet he tells us in the Preface to his book *England under the Tudors* how he constructed his analysis of Tudor England around certain aspects of the subject which seemed most important to him:

> Tudor history can be written round such topics as religion, the maritime expansion, or Shakespeare, but I have chosen the constitutional problems of politics and government, in part because they attract me most and in part because I think that they involve less omission or falsification by emphasis than any other central theme.[1]

Elton's choice thus reflects, first, his interests (Tudor constitutional history is his main field of research); and, secondly, his judgement. What we are reading about is Tudor England analysed not 'on its own terms' (whatever that could possibly mean in practice) but on terms set, inevitably and legitimately, by the author. Other historians, with equal legitimacy, have analysed the period in different terms, according to *their* interests and judgement. How could it be otherwise?

But professional historians – Professor Elton prominent among them[2] – would argue that *England under the Tudors*, being a general work, cannot be regarded as 'real' history. In their view, as we have seen, 'real' history is the learned monograph or article resting upon original research; only a small fraction of a general work or text-book can have such a foundation. We are confronted here with a most revealing aspect of the professional approach: that 'real' history is what professional historians write for each other, not what they write for educated laymen in society at large, a category which – it cannot be emphasised too often – includes the great majority of their students. However, apart from the fact that *England under the Tudors* reflects to a considerable degree its author's research interests, even the learned monograph or article involves *reconstruction* of the past by the historian and not merely its *recovery* as the professional approach suggests. The

[1] *England under the Tudors* (1962), p. v.
[2] For example, in *The English Historical Review*, vol. lxxxvi (1971), p. 217, Elton speaks of 'the "real" history of the monograph' as distinct from 'general works and textbooks'.

past does not lie ready to hand in documents waiting for historians to recover it. Only at the most minute and elementary level of textual analysis can the historian's activity be said to be outside his control: he cannot falsify the text. And to consider this as 'real' history is to reduce the discipline to the mere exercise of its auxiliary skills.

Above that level the present circumstances of the historian become a vital element in his reconstruction of the past which is history. For history is not 'the past', nor yet the surviving past. It is a reconstruction of certain parts of the past (from surviving evidence) which in some way have had relevance for the present circumstances of the historian who reconstructed them. And this is irrefutably so, whether the historian was motivated by a burning curiosity about some particular subject or period; was recommended a certain field of study as a student by his professor (a recommendation much influenced by the availability of documents); or chanced upon a collection of hitherto unexamined documents and built an academic career upon them – to mention but three of the various circumstances in which surviving evidence and historians come together. At every stage, present circumstances dictate the terms upon which the meeting between historians and the past takes place; the initiative in the process can come only from the former. The historian has to decide what he wants to know from the surviving materials. His 'facts' are those he uses because they have some relevance for his field of enquiry.

The historian cannot separate his study of the past from his present circumstances. It has been well observed that 'there will always be a connection between the way in which men contemplate the past and the way in which they contemplate the present'.[1] Moreover, the historian is a part of society from whose current moods and values he cannot disassociate himself. This point has been brilliantly made by the Dutch historian, Pieter Geyl, in demonstrating how the judgements of successive French historians upon Napoleon over the nineteenth century reflected the changing trends in French political life and thought during that period. Geyl's study also demonstrates the essentially interim character of historical judgements. Equally significant, and adding further point to the argument, is Geyl's approach to the problem of assessing Napoleon, in which the conscious parallel with

[1] T. H. Buckle, quoted in Marwick, op. cit., p. 21.

Hitler, and his own wartime experience – as he himself states[1] –
were so influential. It is also interesting to note that Professor Sir
Herbert Butterfield, whom I have already quoted as a firm
advocate of the need to divorce the present from the past,[2] was
moved in the patriotic climate of the Second World War period to
write approvingly of the concept of a *marriage* between the present
and the past.[3] And why not? Historians themselves change. They
mature (and decline); they live and write history in a changing
world. These facts of life are bound to be reflected in what they
write.

In spite of its inherent weaknesses – and what can only be
described as delusions upon which it is so largely based – the
professional approach continues not merely to survive but to
dominate the practice of history. This is not as surprising as
might be thought at first glance. Once history was established in
the universities, sheltered from the outside world, a class of
professional historians grew up which was able to determine the
manner in which the discipline should be conducted. These men,
imbued with the concept of scientific history, believed that the
autonomy and status of history as an academic discipline were
bound up with the scholarly techniques they had developed to
establish from surviving documents what had happened in the
past. They have come to constitute a self-perpetuating group,
absorbing into their ranks others whom they have fashioned in
their own image.

Insight into this process may be gained by observing the way
in which a professional historian is made. A young postgraduate
student undertakes research into some part of the surviving past
upon the recommendation, and with the advice, of his professor
or tutor, both established historians. The latter will help him to
choose a 'good research topic', the most important factor in such
a choice being the availability of documents rather than the
importance of the particular historical situation to which they
relate. A young historian's initial research is normally undertaken
in order to obtain a doctoral degree, which will give him the
credentials for becoming a professional: the Ph.D. has been
described most aptly as a union card. It involves the candidate

---

[1] *Napoleon: For and Against* (paperback edn., 1965), pp. 7–10.
[2] See above, p. 35.
[3] *The Englishman and His History* (1944), pp. 4–5.

in working on a narrow, and therefore manageable, subject. He is concerned, at this stage, primarily with mastering techniques and acquiring expertise; though he is working upon and expanding, however modestly, the frontiers of knowledge. For the young scholar this is exacting, but generally enjoyable, work. When it is complete he has reconstructed some small part of the past; he is a trained historian and, if he can obtain an academic post, a professional.

His immediate audience is a small group of professional historians appointed to examine his doctoral thesis. He must now seek to widen his audience to include a larger number of professionals who may be interested in the subject of his research. He will do this by producing articles for the learned (that is, professional) journals and writing scholarly books. If he is fortunate his thesis, with little modification and additional research, will become his first book. He will be very unfortunate indeed if it cannot yield at least one or two learned articles. His objective is to establish himself as an authority in the field in which he has been conducting his research: to establish himself, that is, in the judgement of his colleagues, especially the more senior ones. For these are the men who hold key positions for his future: who edit the learned journals, advise reputable publishing houses on their academic publications, and, most importantly, appoint young scholars – fashioned in their own image – to their own ranks as university teachers of history. The relevance of his research to the professional historian needs no further emphasis: his career is bound up with it, and so is much of his intellectual capital. Thus a young scholar becomes a professional historian, conducting research and publishing the results for an audience of his fellow professionals. With them he helps to determine the terms upon which the past is reconstructed. It is extremely important to note that the criteria by which *teaching* appointments are made to university departments of history are thus those of historical scholarship as interpreted by professional historians.

We have just seen how a young historian embarks upon his career by mastering techniques of historical scholarship and displaying the expertise he has acquired in a narrow field of historical research. So he learns his trade. But instead of proceeding to apply himself to the investigation of broader and more significant historical matters, he more often than not continues his research on similarly narrow lines. It has been truly observed that 'few men, thoroughly soaked in the waters of one historical pond, feel inclined to swim in another'.[1] Thus is the development of the historian arrested as he continues to apply his stereotyped techniques to more and more documents without reference to the historical relevance of their contents: that is, their significance to the changing circumstances of human society. He is thus encouraged by the professional approach, which itself embodies the arrested development of the discipline since the enthronement of scientific history. We saw how the followers of Ranke stopped short at 'a rudimentary level of first-stage positivism' and made the establishment of the facts of history an end in itself. But the number of such facts capable of being established has multiplied immeasurably. Only by trying to arrest history at some point in time at which the amount of surviving material ceases to be manageable can historians committed to the professional approach hope to deal with it.

We have long since passed that point. A situation of there being too few surviving documents to enable the historian to arrive at satisfactory answers to significant questions has given way to one in which there are too many for him to cope with. We still cannot discover everything about the past, but it now becomes impossible to deny the necessity for selection even from its surviving traces. Unfeignedly, we have to decide what aspects of it are relevant to our present interests and needs; what questions we want the evidence to help us answer, rather than what information it can yield. For the potential amount of information is otherwise far too great for us to contend with. But surely, in principle as well as in practice, this is what the historian's approach should always be. We no more want to know everything that happened in the past than we are interested in everything that is going on at present. Just wanting to know about the past is the mark not of an historian, but of an antiquarian. The professional historian who insists that the past be studied for its own sake regardless of its relevance for us in the present, and who maintains that all aspects of the past are equally worthy of investigation, is making the case for antiquarianism, not for the study of history. The outcome of his approach is that a great deal of the history at present being written is concerned with narrow, highly specialised topics; is

[1] Elton, *The Practice of History,* op. cit., p. 94, n. 7.

written by professionals for professionals; and indicates a preoccupation with minute and esoteric detail at the expense – indeed, to the exclusion – rather than in the service of, broader issues. Unless these detailed studies can be related to issues of wider significance – and reach a wider audience – it is difficult to see their relevance for anyone but the persons who write them and a handful of other specialists. In my view, here may lie an explanation of why such historians oppose the idea of relevance: it threatens the manner in which they set about their work.

The truth is that many professional historians are interested in the past at the expense of a proper concern with the issues of contemporary society. It has been well observed that 'many historians choose their scholarly vocation with the express purpose of loosening their ties with the world they live in'.[1] This is further demonstrated in their pursuit of subjects which have no immediate bearing upon their present interests and experience. There is an element of escapism here. Historians spend their professional lives in analysing the activities, recorded in documents, of past generations of men and women whose present counterparts hold not the slightest interest for them. The world of documents and the world of living people rarely are allowed to intrude upon each other. This situation supports Descartes' assertion (quoted by Lloyd in the previous chapter[2]) that 'when one is too curious about things which were practised in past centuries, one is usually very ignorant about those which are practised in our own time'. But, of course, the professional approach, stressing the need to divorce the past from the present, makes a virtue of such ignorance. It is therefore not surprising to find professional historians freely admitting to it. One such is J. H. Hexter, a prominent American historian. In describing 'his day', Professor Hexter contrasts his unorganised thinking about current problems with the 'orderly, systematic, purposeful way' he conducts his historical research:

> I know practically nothing for sure about the relation of the institutions of higher education in America to the social structure, but I know a fair bit about the relation between the two in France, England and the Netherlands in the fifteenth and sixteenth centuries. I have never studied the Economic

[1] M. M. Postan, *Fact and Relevance: Essays on Historical Method* (1971), p. 56.
[2] See above, p. 16.

Reports to the President that would enable me to appraise the state of the American nation in the 1950s, but I have studied closely the *Discourse of the Commonwealth of England* and derived from it some reasonably coherent notions about the condition of England in the 1550s.[1]

For Hexter, then, the condition of England in the fifteen-fifties had more interest than the condition of his own country at the time he was writing this particular essay (the nineteen-fifties). In other words, it had greater – clearly far greater – relevance for him.

Professor Hexter's sympathy with the professional approach may also be seen in his contemptuous reference in the same essay to 'the chronic do-gooder, who believes that knowledge justifies itself only by a capacity to solve current problems'.[2] More recently, he has criticised those (presumably students) who want history to be relevant to what they judge to be *their* interests:

> If final explanations [of historical phenomena] are very un-
> likely, all of us [professional historians] can at least look
> forward to the continuing intellectual employment of offering
> provisional ones, although obviously the "irrelevance" for
> the Now Generation of anything prior to the Vietnam War
> is about to reduce us all to technological unemployment.[3]

Whether a study of social problems in sixteenth-century England is a more valuable intellectual exercise than a study of the origins of the Vietnam War is a matter of opinion; and any judgement upon this matter would be a value judgement. Both subjects are susceptible to historical analysis. Perhaps Professor Hexter is unaware that there have been hostilities in Vietnam for over a quarter of a century, and that a searching historical analysis of the present conflict would take us much further back into the past. However, the point is that it is perfectly legitimate for young American history students, who – presumably unlike Professor Hexter – could be personally involved in the Vietnam War, to find relevance in studying the historical background to it rather than in concerning themselves with the problems of Tudor England. Hexter's remarks, and their tone, suggest an uncomfortable

[1] *Reappraisals in History* (1961), p. 9.
[2] Ibid., p. 1.
[3] 'Postscript to an Awfully Long Review', *The Journal of British Studies*, vol. ix, no. 1 (November 1969), p. 48.

awareness that the demand of others that history should have relevance for *them* threatens the professional historian's present privilege of practising history in a way that has relevance for *him*.

Who are these others, and what are the professional historian's obligations to them? They are first the society of which he is a part; and, secondly, and more specifically, the university students whom society employs him to teach. Let us look first at society. And we must note at the outset the historian's claim that society 'needs' history.[1] If this is indeed so, it certainly is not the 'real' history of the learned journals; nor does society need to keep professional historians in what Professor Hexter would presumably call (most aptly in my opinion) 'technological employment'. A special attribute of history used to be its attraction for laymen. But the professional approach – as we have seen – inevitably divorces the historian from his wider audience. Its emphasis upon the particular, at the expense of larger issues; its narrow specialisation and lack of broad perspectives; and, perhaps above all, its preoccupation with quasi-technicalities, elevating means above ends – these tendencies have led the professional historian to turn away from educated laymen and to concentrate upon writing for a narrow circle of his fellows.

The growth of professionalism has not gone uncriticised. A number of distinguished historians have drawn attention to its dangers. In the lecture to which I have already referred,[2] Professor Trevor-Roper spoke of 'the creeping paralysis of professionalism'.[3] In his Presidential Address to the Diamond Jubilee Conference of the Historical Association in 1966, Professor Geoffrey Barraclough warned against regarding history 'from a narrowly professional point of view' and reminded his listeners that, in an address thirty-five years earlier, Sir Maurice Powicke had 'protested against the "arid professionalism which regards history as made for the historian" instead of the historian being made for history'.[4] Nor, incidentally, has this concern been confined to British historians. For example, Professor José Honório Rodrigues, the eminent Brazilian historian, has spoken of 'a crisis in historical thought. This crisis is due not only to

[1] For example, Marwick, op. cit., p. 12: 'Quite simply, human society *needs* history' (Marwick's italics).
[2] See above, p. 39.
[3] *History: Professional and Lay*, op. cit., p. 18.
[4] *History and the Common Man* (1967), pp. 4–5.

specialization, which digs ever deeper into the dark well of the particularity and singularity of events, but also to the fact that the audience is increasingly being limited to professional historians.'[1]

But professionalism continues to flourish, and ever more strongly. It is dominant in historical periodicals, which withdraw with every issue further and further into realms of esoteric expertise, far removed from the interest and understanding of educated laymen. *The English Historical Review* is an outstanding example. Looking at it today it is difficult to credit that when it was launched in 1886 its promoters expressed an intention to cater for the general reader as well as for the professional historian. *Past & Present*, which began publication in 1952:

> is designed to reach an audience that includes both specialists and non-specialists; to communicate the results of historical research in readable and lively form; to provide a forum for debate in which historians and scholars in allied subjects take part and to encourage the examination of particular problems and periods for the light they throw on wider issues of historical change.

Regrettably, the limited range of articles submitted to it by professional historians has inhibited the fulfilment of these admirable aims.[2] *History Today*, which does cater for educated laymen, is regarded as much less prestigious by professional historians, for whom the learned journals are vehicles for displaying their scholarship, adding to their lists of publications, and thus advancing their careers.

In my judgement, society at large may reasonably demand two main things from the professional historian: satisfaction of its curiosity about the past, and some guidance on present issues and problems. Both have a bearing upon the way in which the historian should present his reconstruction of the past. I would not altogether agree with A. J. P. Taylor's opinion that 'No historian is worth his salt who has not felt some twinge of Macaulay's ambition – to replace the latest novel on the lady's

---

[1] 'History Belongs to Our Own Generation', in Lewis Hanke (ed.), *History of Latin American Civilization: Sources and Interpretations*, vol. 2, *The Modern Age* (1967), p. 496. I have discussed historical matters with Professor Rodrigues at the Biblioteca Nacional in Rio de Janeiro.

[2] See the editor's comment, '*Past and Present* Numbers 1–50', in the fiftieth issue (February 1971), p. 3.

dressing-table',[1] if this implies that the layman reads history merely for entertainment. But I would maintain that the historian should strive to combine accuracy (as far as he can establish it) with literary excellence, if only from the point of view of his lay audience.[2] It is deeply to be regretted that there should be, on the one hand, so much time devoted to work that reaches such a limited audience, and, on the other, so much superficial work enjoying a far wider readership. The professional approach encourages historians to rest content with satisfying what they regard as standards of scholarship. It does not stimulate them to cultivate readability, even on those occasions when they treat subjects having wide lay appeal. In the matter of guidance, there is a strong tendency among professional historians to disclaim any special competence to offer this. Emphasising the particular character of historical events, they are reluctant to affirm (if not vehement in denying) that 'lessons' may be learned from studying them. Nor would I advocate, for a moment, that the study of history should concern itself directly with formulating solutions to contemporary problems. But if historical knowledge does not deepen his understanding of the present, and at least suggest guidelines for the future, the layman may be forgiven for considering the study of history irrelevant to his needs. This means that the historian is abdicating the field to others less reticent in staking their claims to be heard on matters considered urgent by laymen.

There are further – and, in my view, compelling – reasons why the professional historian should maintain a continuing dialogue, and debate, with his lay audience. They concern his obligations, not to society, but to his subject. For, I believe, such a dialogue and debate will help eradicate the weaknesses of the professional approach and enable the historian to make a distinctive contribution to the education and cultural life of his society. I would suggest three specific ways in which addressing himself to laymen as well as to his fellows can be of inestimable value to the professional historian: in weaning him away from his narrow specialisation and making him face up to the broader issues; in improving the literary presentation of his work; and in exposing

---

[1] *Rumours of Wars* (1952), p. 8.
[2] Cf. Lloyd's remarks upon 'the respective claims of accuracy and literary effect' among classical historians and subsequently. See above, chapter 1.

him and his discipline to the critical appraisal of non-professionals. Let us consider each of them in turn.

It cannot be doubted that over-specialisation is a major weakness of the professional approach. For it produces narrowness, not breadth of vision; more learning than understanding. History for its own sake – as I have stressed – becomes the exhaustive study of some fragment from the past for *its* own sake, with scant reference to the wider context in which alone it can have significance. Moreover, excessive concern with detail encourages pedantry more than it develops judgement – a fundamental purpose of studying history as I shall show more fully in the next chapter. Of course attention to detail is essential to sound scholarship. But it is not an end in itself: it is merely the beginning of the historian's task. There is no purpose in crawling upon a narrow sector of the frontiers of knowledge unless one *regularly* stands up to survey the general landscape.[1] There is no surer way of losing perspective – another fundamental of historical work, to which again I will return – than through unremitting preoccupation with the minute and the esoteric. It is vital to distinguish between what is necessary to train an apprentice historian and what is the proper task for the trained professional; and it is my contention that the latter fails to justify his training if he continues (as often he does) to work within that brief period of history upon which he embarked as a postgraduate student. Such specialisation may win him the esteem of his fellows; and, ominously, venturing into other fields may incur their wrath:

> Today most professional historians 'specialise'. They choose a period, sometimes a very brief period, and within that period they strive, in desperate competition with ever-expanding evidence, to know all the facts. Thus armed, they can comfortably shoot down any amateurs who blunder or rivals who stray into their heavily fortified field; and, of course, knowing the strength of modern defensive weapons, they themselves keep prudently within their own frontiers.[2]

But this kind of specialisation is a positive deterrent to a greater understanding of what the whole thing is about – and this is what

---

[1] Cf. Elton, *The Practice of History*, op. cit., p. 34. Elton concedes that 'Perhaps one may want some man at times to stand up, gaze around, and look beyond'.

[2] H. R. Trevor-Roper, *Historical Essays* (1957), pp. v–vi. Incidentally, Trevor-Roper has been much less prudent than most professional historians in this respect.

interests the layman, not the abstruse controversies in which the professionals appear to delight among themselves. In addressing himself to laymen the professional historian will be forced to face up to the larger issues which, in any case, should be his proper concern.

Addressing himself to this wider audience also has a beneficial effect upon the professional historian's presentation of his subject which, it cannot be stressed too often, exists not for the training of professionals but for the education of laymen. History is not a technical subject, and must be preserved from developing the kind of jargon which characterises so many of its present rivals among the social sciences. Let there be no mistake: the combination of literary excellence with scholarly standards is far from easy to achieve. It is much harder to write lucidly for laymen without lowering the intellectual level of one's argument than to compose a learned article for a professional journal, where emphasis is placed upon the number and accuracy of footnote references rather than upon clarity of expression. It has been well said that 'easy reading means hard writing'.[1] Nor can it be doubted that the effort involved is salutary in clarifying the historian's thoughts; involuted writing may equally reflect confusion of mind as weight of learning. At all events such writing has no merit of itself and can only diminish the value of the writer's contribution to historical knowledge. More important still, it has grave consequences for history as a medium of education.[2]

The third, and not least important, benefit which the professional historian derives from a dialogue with laymen lies in its exposing him to the critical judgement of non-professionals. I realise that many professional historians would not regard this as a 'benefit', and indeed already view with something akin to indignation those from outside their ranks who presume to pass judgement upon them. This attitude is mistaken. It is pressure from outside that forces the historian critically to examine fundamental questions about his subject in relation to the changing circumstances of the society to which he belongs. Left to the devices of his own narrow circle, he lacks incentive to consider and to reassess the nature, purposes and methods of his

[1] And the converse is equally true. As Sheridan expressed it, 'easy writing's vile hard reading' (*Clio's Protest*).

[2] These consequences are discussed in chapter 4.

work: to ponder the profound question 'what is the distinctive contribution of your subject to the intellectual and cultural needs of society?' and scorn the   ...icial 'what is your period?'. The dialogue through whic ..lône the professional historian can make his proper contribution both within the university and to the wider needs of society, and thus maintain the vitality of his subject, represents a formidable challenge. But it is a challenge he cannot ignore, if for no worthier reason than that he and his subject are coming under increasing scrutiny from outside: a scrutiny which is one facet of the growing integration of the universities with the life of the community. The days when historians, sheltered in their cloisters, could disdain the idea of their subject being useful and relevant are numbered, like those of so many of our traditional ideas in the academic (as in the wider) world. The relevance of history has to be demonstrated.

Now let us consider the professional historian's obligations to those members of society who form his immediate audience: the university students he is paid to teach. And it must be noted at the outset that, although he owes his position to the presumed relevance of his subject as a medium of education, the professional historian seldom is a trained teacher, and generally lacks expertise as an educator. This leads him to make the comfortable assumption that the exposure of students to his scholarship (and, of course, that of his colleagues) is itself an educative process. This would be an unsatisfactory approach even were the objective of teaching history to train more professional historians: a preposterous idea which nevertheless appears to have its adherents. But the aim of university education, of which history forms a part, is to equip men and women for their lives in the world. The teaching of history should be explicitly relevant to this purpose. The world into which the present generation of students will emerge at the end of their university careers will be different, but not divorced, from the one faced by previous generations. History's concern is with promoting the awareness and understanding, and with developing the judgement, of successive generations in relation to the changing circumstances of human society. These considerations should govern the study of history at university.

The professional approach is not sympathetic to this viewpoint because of the latter's emphasis upon the needs of those who study it rather than upon the autonomy of the subject. Yet although, in the matter of research, the professional tends to reject the idea of a hierarchy of worth, he does give preference in the syllabus to the traditional fields of English and (to a lesser degree) European history. A main argument in favour of these fields is the availability of materials for studying them, and the chief argument advanced against the study of African, Asian and Latin American history is the comparative lack of 'documents' or their non-availability. The case for concentrating very largely upon English history is strongly argued by Professor Elton, even to the extent of impugning the motives of those who disagree with this view.[1] But he seems to forget that the emphasis hitherto placed upon English constitutional history – which, understandably, he wishes to maintain – derives from *its* relevance at a time when the world (and, above all, Britain's place in it) was very different.[2] Of course, 'there is no proof that a knowledge of history, recent or distant, at B.A. level succeeds in giving a man much understanding of his own time.'[3] Indeed, I am greatly concerned that the study of history well beyond the first degree level only too often appears not to do so either. This I attribute, not to the nature of the subject, but to the shortcomings of the professional approach, which rejects the idea of relevance and tries to divorce the past from the present. If the study of history does not give us a greater understanding of the present, this is an excellent reason for revising our approach.

I am not concerned here with history syllabuses as such, still less with actual teaching methods, but again with approach. For the professional historian – as I have tried to show – the study of history has relevance at least in terms of the satisfaction he himself

---

[1] '. . . I find the frequent attacks on English history in English schools of history hard to understand; or rather, I should find them hard to understand if I thought that the attackers were pursuing intellectual ends rather than political and social – were concerned to train reasoning intelligences rather than produce supposedly desirable beings – worthy citizens of the world, admirers of the United Nations, or even Friends of the Soviet Union' (*The Practice of History*, op. cit., p. 198). If this passage is not sufficient to raise doubts about Professor Elton's own 'intellectual ends', the reader is referred to Elton's Inaugural Lecture, *The Future of the Past*, op. cit., p. 22: 'There is still a great deal to be said for living in this country, and the historian's task consists among other things, if I may so put it, in a crude re-kindling of a certain respect for a country whose past justifies that respect.'

[2] This point is made, significantly, in *Towards World History* (Department of Education and Science, Education Pamphlet Number 52, 1967), p. 9.

[3] *The Practice of History*, op. cit., p. 185.

derives from it. But as a teacher he has to demonstrate its relevance for his students, whose approach and needs, in the main, are different from his. The common ground between them, upon which the teacher has to build, is their shared experience of living in the present world; and therefore the professional approach, which eschews the present and seeks to withdraw from it, can only be an obstacle to effective teaching. In practice the present cannot be ignored, but the historian who attempts to set present problems aside will, if nothing else, diminish his means of communicating with his students, the most lively of whom will be concerned with these matters and indeed should be encouraged in this respect by their historical studies. Moreover, knowledge of present issues can give valuable insight into problems of the past: a point which will be developed further in the next chapter.

Another aspect of the professional approach which tends to divorce the historian from his students is research. In principle, the historian should receive from pursuing research intellectual stimulus that in turn should make him a more stimulating teacher. Furthermore, his work on the frontiers of knowledge should enable him to demonstrate to his students the process of reconstructing the past and, beyond that, his own contribution towards promoting understanding of such broader issues as might stimulate them. But, as I have shown, a great deal of historical research is concentrated in ever smaller detail upon 'the particular', with scant reference to wider issues. This essential characteristic of the professional approach to the study of history, stressing the subject's concern with the particular character of events, is often paraded as a virtue. But its effect is to widen the communications gap between the professional and laymen, including the majority of his students. The professional historian may believe that he can apply himself successfully to the study of particular situations in isolation from general issues. In my judgement, he deceives himself by believing so. But certainly, for students and laymen alike, the minutiae of history are incomprehensible unless they are related, deliberately, explicitly, and indeed unremittingly to broader circumstances that are meaningful to them. In practice, rather than drawing inspiration from their research to enrich their teaching, many historians find their two activities less and less compatible with each other, and come to regard the former as their 'private work'. Research, far from being a source of enrichment for university teaching, becomes a rival claimant for the historian's time. In terms of both intellectual satisfaction and material reward (through the advancement of their careers) it tends, understandably, to have a stronger attraction for many university teachers of history. It is a common complaint among students that their teachers are more interested in their own research than in them.

Most important of all, the professional historian tends – unconsciously perhaps rather than deliberately – to encourage his students to adopt his own approach to the study of history. Consequently, emphasis is laid upon the compilation of facts rather than upon the asking of questions. As it is, students come up to university trained principally to memorise so-called facts of history and need, above all, to be taught to ask relevant questions. Unfortunately, the professional historian who spends a great part of his career in extracting the maximum number of 'facts' from manuscripts is ill-fitted to discourage his students from spending a great deal of their time in compiling large quantities of information – relevant or otherwise – from books; or from reproducing such information indiscriminately in their essays and examination answers. It has been well said that 'A mere collector of supposed facts is as useful as a collector of matchboxes'.[1] I must add that most collectors of matchboxes I have known have seemed to derive a great deal of happiness, and even excitement, from their hobby; while too many students reading history appear bored, and distressingly few excited, by the subject.[2] This last is itself sufficient reason for a critical reappraisal of what we are about.

I would like in concluding this chapter to summarise the points I have made in criticism of the professional approach to the study and writing of history, and so pave the way for the formulation of a fresh approach which I believe necessary to prevent the decline of the subject implicit in the present situation. My contention has been that the professional approach is deleterious to history as an intellectual pursuit; to the performance of its

[1] Lucien Febvre, quoted by Marwick, op. cit., p. 245.

[2] See, for example, the assertion in 1963 in the journal *Cambridge Opinion* that 'a very large proportion of those reading history are bored by their subject' (quoted by A. J. Taylor, *History in an Age of Growth* (1964), p. 6). According to the editor of *History* (vol. liii (1968), p. 389) the subject is thought by the pupils of many teachers of history 'to be boring and irrelevant'.

potentially significant social function; and, most importantly, to its role as a medium of education. I have indicated how the professional approach has failed even by its own criteria (misguided as I judge these to be) and has long since ceased to be relevant to the circumstances either of the discipline itself or of the society in which it is practised. In pursuing autonomy and status as an academic discipline for their subject, historians have abandoned the traditional qualities which have made history attractive to laymen, in favour of a sterile professionalism which denies in practice what are claimed as its objectives in theory. What professionals are doing may have relevance for them, but it is largely irrelevant to the needs of society as a whole, and is a positive obstacle to a realisation of the subject's potential as a medium of education.

The fundamental weakness of the professional approach to history as an intellectual pursuit lies in certain assumptions – patently, delusions – upon which it rests. It is not possible to divorce 'the past' from 'the present', either in principle – since time is a constantly moving frontier – or in practice, in terms of separating the historian's analysis of surviving documents from his present circumstances. It can no longer seriously be contended that what historians are doing will one day (however remote) make possible a definitive, universal history. Yet historians continue to accumulate information about the past as if this were still their objective; hence their emphasis upon professional skills in order to extract this information from documents. They have equated the application of technical expertise with historical scholarship, and have made this their major occupation rather than the development of judgement through the comparative evaluation of historical phenomena. They have reduced a subject concerned with the totality of human experience to fragments whose sum represents a minute and ever diminishing fraction of the whole.

The professional approach derives from an identifiable set of historical circumstances, as Lloyd showed in the first chapter. In the intellectual climate of that period it was possible for professional historians to convince themselves of the feasibility of establishing what happened in the past through the scientific analysis of surviving documents. At the same time, since documents appeared to be limited, they could also believe it necessary to extract every conceivable 'fact' from them. But this situation has long since ceased to exist. There are masses of documents: far too many for the historian to cope with and yet far too few to achieve his supposed objective. The prime task of the historian is to select from the vast amount of material now available to him. What he needs in his present situation is not so much technical expertise in interpreting every precious document upon which he can lay his hands, as mature judgement in formulating the questions he wants answered. In developing such judgement he will need the widest possible experience – from the world of living men as much as from the world of documents. For, as Marc Bloch, the eminent French historian, declared:

> Misunderstanding of the present is the inevitable conse-
> quence of ignorance of the past. But a man may wear himself
> out just as fruitlessly in seeking to understand the past, if he
> is totally ignorant of the present . . . [The] faculty of under-
> standing the living is, in very truth, the master quality of the
> historian.[1]

Few historians possess such a faculty. The professional approach expressly discourages its cultivation.

The historian must recognise that the past cannot be studied for its own sake and on its own terms, nor can it be divorced from the present. History is not the recovery of 'the past'; it is a reconstruction of some parts of the past undertaken by historians for whom in some way they have had relevance. Moreover, it is impossible for an historian to reconstruct any part of the past 'as it was'. His reconstruction inevitably would be unrecognisable to the people who actually experienced the events he has tried to reconstruct, could they see it. It is the historian's task to give to an historical situation a degree of coherence of which the people involved were quite unaware. But, of course, he is not re-constructing the past for their benefit, but for ours in the present. The study of history is concerned with the relationship between past events and living men. And, in my judgement, far from viewing the intrusion of the present as a source of weakness in their studies, historians should recognise it as an essential dimen-sion of their discipline. Otherwise, what they are practising is at best antiquarianism.

[1] *The Historian's Craft* (1954), p. 43.

The professional historian must also realise that his concern with his subject's autonomy is a source not of strength, but of weakness. For it has led him to stress his technical expertise, when his is not a technical subject. Faced with a growing challenge from other disciplines, especially certain of the social sciences, the historian has tended to ape their techniques and even their jargon, often with a view to scientific appearances.[1] Thus the effect of professional historians' insistence upon the autonomy of their subject is counter-productive. It makes history merely one academic discipline amongst many others. But history is very different from other disciplines. The difference lies in its embracing every aspect of human activity, including those other disciplines. Its role in relation to them is an interpretative one. History relates to each other, in space and time, various other disciplines which in turn relate to different aspects of human activity. This gives it special value to educated laymen. The concern of history with the whole of human experience – vitiated by the professional approach and its concentration upon the particular – has important implications for the subject as a medium of education, which are considered later in the book.

Reluctant to come to terms with the new situation, historians who adhere to the professional approach seem to want the process of history to stand still so that they can go on as before, undisturbed by the great changes in society which have transformed the environment in which their subject is studied. Absorbed in their own specialised fields they seldom concern themselves with fundamental questions in regard to their discipline. They appear quite happy to go on adding to the store of historical knowledge or working over the old problems, offering interim judgements upon them *ad infinitum*. There is plenty to keep them in 'technological employment'. Hence their emotive response to demands that the study of history should be relevant to a changed – and rapidly changing – situation. This from practitioners of a discipline avowedly concerned with change in human society![2]

[1] For example, the susceptibility of historians to the techniques – and indeed the jargon – of economists may be clearly seen in the pages of *The Economic History Review*.

[2] For example, Elton, *The Practice of History*, op. cit., p. 22, declares that the historian 'will have to concentrate on understanding change, which is the essential content of historical analysis and description'.

The attitude of professional historians to the society of which they form a part is ambivalent. On the one hand, they claim that history has an important social function: society needs history. Yet, as we have seen, they reserve 'real' history for each other. If society needs history, its needs are not met by professional historians, whose concentration upon the particular divorces them from the wider audience which is concerned with the larger issues. Moreover, not only are professional historians suspicious of colleagues who work upon the whole process of history: they are at least equally suspicious of those who are 'popular' – that is, write history having wide lay appeal. In any case the emphasis placed by professional historians upon their role as scholars marks them off as a little community insulated from society at large. But the little community in which they exist itself has a social function: one of the most important in our society, that of education.

For most important of all are the implications of the professional approach for history as a medium of education. Education is concerned with preparing people for their lives in the world: their lives in a changing society. Historians who deliberately turn their backs on their present circumstances in order – as they believe – to increase their understanding of the past could hardly be more ill-equipped to help others to cope with living in today's world. In their hands university education appears to be a means of enabling young people to spend three or four years insulated from society and its problems; and by the same token, of enabling scholars to spend their whole professional lives in this fashion. I have already indicated some of the unhappy consequences of the university teacher of history's being so inexpert as an educator. But this is not all. For not only do professional historians determine the way history is taught in the universities, but they powerfully influence the way it is taught in schools and colleges.[1] With professional historians so absorbed in the compilation of historical facts, it is hardly surprising that the memorisation of historical information is what so often passes for history in our schools – and universities. These matters are fully discussed by Lloyd in chapter four.

The demand for relevance may be a threat to the professional approach, but it is a challenge to the discipline, and an opportunity: an opportunity for historians to reaffirm the traditional

[1] See above, pp. 3–4.

qualities of the subject and to bring its practice back into the service of society. It means, above all, harmonising the roles of history as an intellectual pursuit, as a social function and as a medium of education. It entails a fresh approach, which I would call a 'contemporary approach', because its point of departure is not the past, but the insistent present. Its central concern is with people and not with documents. Its aim is not just to establish what happened in the past, as if this were an end in itself, but to assess the contemporary – and therefore ever changing – significance of historical phenomena. It encourages involvement in our rapidly changing society, and not escape from it. It emphasises history as a medium of education and instruction for laymen, and not as the preserve of scholars dedicated to a study of the past regardless of its relevance to the rest of society which supports their activities. The formulation of such a contemporary approach is the principal concern of the next chapter.

3 *A Contemporary Approach*

THE purpose of this chapter is to formulate an approach to the practice of history appropriate to the present, rapidly changing circumstances of our discipline, of the institutions in which it is practised, and of society at large: in short, a contemporary approach. Such an approach will be relevant to the historian's role as scholar, citizen and teacher. As an essential preliminary I shall consider the significance of 'contemporary history', and the attitude of many professional historians towards this sector of their discipline. My consideration will involve, first of all, an examination of the main arguments usually advanced against the study of contemporary history, demonstrating the false premises upon which these very largely are based and how they serve to confirm weaknesses and contradictions in the professional approach already analysed. Although my purpose is to formulate a contemporary approach, and not to make the case for studying contemporary history as such, I shall indicate the latter's special contribution to historical studies as a whole, in terms both of scholarship and of education.

We must note at the outset the substantial opposition which exists among professional historians to the very notion of contemporary history: it is almost as if the phrase were a contradiction in terms. This opposition indicates an identification of 'contemporary' with 'the present' and of 'history' with 'the past', thus reflecting that attempt to divorce the past from the present which – as I have shown – is such an important feature of the professional approach. Clearly, it is untenable. For, since there exists no meaningful division between the past and the present, there can be no terminal date set for the study of history: no point at which acceptable modern history ends, and an unacceptable contemporary period begins. Moreover, it must never be overlooked that, whatever their fields of study, all historians are working on a constantly moving frontier. However, what is normally meant by contemporary history is, in practice, recent or very recent history, which many historians understand to be the history of the twentieth century. Although – as Lloyd demonstrated in the first chapter – a great deal of contemporary history (in the sense of what was recent or what was considered to be of contemporary significance at the time the historian wrote it) has been written from the time of Herodotus onwards, many professional historians today argue against the study of recent history as an academic discipline. Sometimes they apply to it the pejorative term 'current affairs' or seek to dismiss it as 'mere journalism'. Their main arguments relate to documents, perspective and bias. Let us consider each in turn.

A major objection made against the writing of contemporary history is the non-availability of what are usually called in this context 'the documents'. On the face of it such an objection appears absurd – which indeed it is – since the contemporary historian has very many documentary sources at his disposal of a kind denied to his colleagues working on earlier periods. One has only to consider, for example, the documentary evidence for events leading up to the signing of the United Nations Charter compared with what we have for the background to Magna Carta. It is an interesting commentary upon the professional approach which – as we have seen – lays such emphasis upon documents, that medieval history, where the documentary materials often are the most limited, should be considered more 'scholarly' than later periods of history where they exist in such abundance. This attitude, as I have already noted, derives from an identification of historical scholarship with the employment of professional expertise rather than with the refinement of judgement. However, within the context of this objection, the phrase 'the documents' refers to classified material which governments will not make available to historians for at least a generation. But the argument that without access to these particular documents no satisfactory historical analysis can be made of recent events is weak for a number of cogent reasons, apart from the fact that a very great deal of apparently acceptable history has been written without comparable materials.

In the first place, all the documents will never be available; as with earlier periods, the evidence will always be incomplete. There has been a growing tendency in recent times – deriving from changes in media of communication upon the one hand, and the increasing preoccupation of governments with security upon the other – to remove relevant information from written records. In this connection, the storage of information in computers has serious implications for historians.[1] Moreover, by no means all the written records are likely to be made available to historians: for example, under the Public Records Act of 1967, which established the thirty-year rule, the Lord Chancellor retains the right to withhold some categories of documents. Even when 'the documents' are made available to historians, and one apparent objection to contemporary history thereby removed, they will still not furnish the means to total reconstruction of past events. In the second place, the reliability of documents of this kind which are put at the disposal of historians is much more questionable than many of the latter appear to assume. It is sometimes forgotten that documents have always been written as often to conceal as to inform – and very few indeed could have been written in order to provide reliable information for a future generation of historians. On the contrary, where the writer of such documents has historians in mind he is likely to be less reliable than otherwise, and for recent history this situation is more prevalent than for earlier periods. With the operation of the thirty-year rule, both the writer and those who figure in his documents (or at least their families) may well be alive when the documents are made available to historians. These documents have to be analysed with quite as much circumspection as the vast amount of material published by governments and individuals specifically to explain and justify current policies. Of the latter – as of documentary materials generally – the contemporary historian has an over-abundance: a point to which I shall return presently.

But whether suffering from the non-availability of certain documents or an over-abundance of others – or both – the historian of any period is never able to examine all the possible evidence and, if only for this reason, cannot make definitive judgements. In 1895 Lord Acton felt able to affirm that:

[1] Nor must the possibility of computers replacing whole 'armies of research students' (see above, p. 39) be overlooked. A modern computer has been described (F. S. Fussner, *Tudor History and the Historians* (1970), p. 5) as 'perhaps the ideal type or model of historical memory'.

> . . . the contemporary differs from the modern in this, that
> many of its facts cannot by us be definitely ascertained. The
> living do not give up their secrets with the candour of the
> dead; one key is always excepted, and a generation passes
> before we can ensure accuracy.[1]

Several generations later no professional historian would seriously
assert that we have 'ensured accuracy' regarding events in 1895,
though we have refined our judgements concerning them.
Indeed, all historical judgements are interim judgements, to be
reassessed and modified in the light of new evidence and changing
perspectives. Those who criticise contemporary history on
account of the incompleteness of the documents appear to
overlook this.

Judgement is importantly linked with perspective; and lack of
perspective is the second main argument offered against the
writing of contemporary history. The contemporary historian, it
seems, is too close to the events he is analysing to be able to bring
historical perspective to bear upon them. This appears to be a
more serious objection – until one looks more closely at what
'perspective' means to historians. Clearly, its chief meaning is not
the interpretation of events in the light of what came afterwards.
According to Professor Elton, the professional historian is
concerned with 'truly understanding an age from the inside –
living with its attitudes and prejudices'.[2] He also declares that
'Perhaps the historian's most difficult handicap – much worse than
any mere prejudice – lies in his inevitable hindsight'.[3] There is an
inescapable contradiction here: if 'hindsight' is 'inevitable' how
can one possibly arrive at true 'understanding' in Elton's sense?
However, in terms of time it would seem that for the historian
perspective chiefly means reconstructing events in the light of
foregoing circumstances. The contemporary historian, to a
degree at least no less than are his other professional colleagues,
is in a position to view the events of his period in the light of what
came before: in other words, he is putting the recent past into
'historical perspective'. But perspective also means viewing events
and situations in relation to other, contemporaneous events and

[1] *Lectures on Modern History* (paperback edn., 1960), p. 18.
[2] *The Practice of History*, op. cit., p. 30.
[3] Ibid., p. 127. In his later book, *Political History: Principles and Practice* (1970),
p. 137, Elton refers to hindsight as 'the essence of historical knowledge'.

situations. Whether professional historians working on earlier periods and aiming to understand them 'from within' are better able than contemporary historians to achieve such a perspective is open to doubt.

This brings me to the question of bias. For just as perspective is importantly linked with judgement, so is bias importantly linked with perspective. Now it is generally assumed that the contemporary historian is more likely to be partisan than are his colleagues working on earlier periods because the issues involved are closer to him personally. But is this necessarily so? Is impartiality a function of remoteness in time? I would suggest that the most obvious bias against which every professional historian constantly must be on his guard is the understandable tendency to inflate the importance of his particular field of research and the significance of his own discoveries within it. Moreover, no historian, however detached he may feel himself to be, can completely exclude from his work either his own personality or the ideas of the society of which he is a member. Complete impartiality in the writing of history just is not possible, however hard we may and should strive to approximate to it.

We should do well to remember that when an historian attempts to reconstruct the past 'from within' he commits himself to another kind of bias. Professor J. B. Black, for example, showed awareness of this in the Preface to his book on the reign of Elizabeth I:

> In the present volume we have been compelled to observe events predominantly through English eyes, or, to be more correct, through the eyes of the English government – to look upon the kings of France and Spain, the popes, Mary Stuart, and James VI as 'problems' to be solved rather than as beings entitled to a separate and sympathetic consideration. But the writer is aware, and the reader ought also to be aware, that there is another point of view which must be taken into account before we begin to speak of objective history in the proper sense of the words. An attempt has been made to keep this in mind while writing the book, but the paramount necessity of placing the reader at the standpoint of the queen and her ministers has prevented a rigorous following out of the principle.[1]

---

[1] *The Reign of Elizabeth, 1558–1603* (2nd edn., 1959), pp. viii–ix.

The 'standpoint' of Queen Elizabeth I finds a stout champion in Professor Elton, who, as we have seen, strongly supports the notion of getting 'within' a period. On one of the 'problems' noted by Professor Black he writes:

> If she [Elizabeth] suspected that later ages, more distant from the problem and therefore better able to take the wrong view, might condemn her for the death of the unfortunate queen of Scots, one hopes she did not let it trouble her.[1]

Experience indicates that an historian may feel as deeply involved in the issues of the Reformation, for example, as of the current war in Indo-China; indeed, given his preoccupation with the past, he may feel more so.

In addition to the personality of the historian there is the bias of the generation to which he belongs. In chapter two I mentioned Pieter Geyl's analysis of the changing views of Napoleon held by French historians during the nineteenth century.[2] Involvement in a situation – and therefore bias – can be felt by generations (at least of historians) long after it has ceased to exist. In the judgement of Dr. C. V. Wedgwood, for example, it is still too soon for historians to write impartially about the English Civil War, because, in her words:

> We are still so much involved with this conflict that passion and propaganda colour all that has been written about it. It is not yet an academic study which we can approach with scientific indifference and cannot become so while a vital current of continuous belief runs through it to us.

She goes on to make the closely related observation:

> The final, dispassionate, authoritative history of the Civil Wars cannot be written until the problems have ceased to matter; by that time it will not be worth writing.[3]

I would paraphrase Miss Wedgwood to read 'have ceased to be relevant'. Relevant history concerns matters of significance for us, which may well imply controversy; and controversy should

---

[1] *England under the Tudors*, op. cit., p. 370. This passage illustrates the views on 'mere prejudice' and 'hindsight' expressed by Elton in the passages I quoted on p. 64.

[2] See above, p. 41.

[3] *The King's Peace, 1637–1641* (paperback edn., 1966), p. 14.

be a powerful factor in the pursuit of understanding. Controversy over vital issues of significance is indeed the lifeblood of history, not 'those technical disputes and controversies in which professional historians are so apt to delight'.[1]

Basically, the task of the contemporary historian does not differ from the one faced by historians working on earlier periods. Like them, he is concerned with the reconstruction of some part of the past, examining his materials critically and interpreting them judiciously. Like them, too, he constantly is modifying and refining his judgements in the light of new evidence and changing perspectives. In certain important respects his task is more exacting than theirs. The problem of selection – which means, above all, asking the right questions – is much more formidable because of the vast quantity of material available to him. His judgements are more open to challenge from practitioners of other disciplines and from laymen, as well as from fellow professionals – and liable to earlier revision. The historian of remoter periods has greater opportunity for irresponsible interpretation because neither his subjects nor their contemporaries are in a position to challenge his views. Over forty years ago Professor R. W. Seton-Watson identified 'a certain salutary check upon the contemporary historian', observing that:

> to-day it is impossible for any reputable historian to risk such a travesty of character – shall we say, for the sake of argument, of President Wilson or Mr. Lloyd George – as that which a great historian of last century perpetrated upon Henry VIII or Mary Queen of Scots . . . To-day those who, encouraged by the wealth of first-hand material already at their disposal, attempt to pass no less summary a judgment on the statesmen of 1918 are at once confronted by a crowd of contemporaries ready to brand them as mere caricaturists.[2]

Of course, such critics are at least as likely as the contemporary historian to be partisan. But barriers in the way of detached evaluation of events and people are normal hazards of the historian's profession. The difference between the contemporary historian and his colleagues working on earlier periods in this respect is, at most, one of degree; and the former may well be

[1] Barraclough, *History and the Common Man*, op. cit., p. 5.
[2] 'A Plea for the Study of Contemporary History', *History, New Series*, vol. xiv 1930), p. 11. The 'great historian' referred to by Seton-Watson was J. A. Froude.

fortified in dealing with such hazards by enhanced awareness of the dangers he faces.

At the same time, he enjoys a number of advantages. Not only has he a richer variety of written materials; he has other sources, such as films and sound recordings, and often he is able to interview leading participants in the events he is analysing. Before considering the interview, I would like to stress the importance of serious and responsible journalism in the writing of contemporary history, especially since it is sometimes said in denigration of the latter that it is 'nothing more than journalism'. The importance of serious newspaper reports on contemporary events to the trained historian is well illustrated by Sir Lewis Namier's *Diplomatic Prelude*, an account of events leading up to the outbreak of the Second World War based to a considerable extent upon them.[1] This book is still significant. Indeed, can it seriously be argued that many of the contemporary chronicles upon which a great deal of medieval history has been based are to be compared as reliable sources of history with, for example, the London *Times*? Writing of the importance of the newspaper as material for history, Professor V. H. Galbraith asserts: 'Its value lies in the fact that it is strictly contemporary. It is not distorted by hindsight.' Moreover, he says, 'despite bias and propaganda, the newspaper gives a mass of factual information unobtainable elsewhere'.[2] I would add another significant point about newspapers: they not only reflect the climate in which political decisions are made, but also help to form it in a way that earlier manuscripts did not. This greatly enhances their value as source materials for historians.

As regards interviewing, this can be very valuable provided the historian is able to frame the right questions: a criterion equally applicable to the examination of documents. 'How much', asks Alan Bullock pertinently, 'would the historian of the Nineteenth century not give to be able to question Metternich or Cavour' as Bullock himself was able 'to discuss with Lord Attlee the history of the post-war Labour Government or with Mr. Acheson the decision to re-arm Germany in 1950'.[3] Of course, to paraphrase

[1] L. B. Namier, *Diplomatic Prelude, 1938–1939* (1948).
[2] *An Introduction to the Study of History* (1964), p. 44.
[3] 'Is it Possible to Write Contemporary History ?', in Max Beloff (ed.), *On the Track of Tyranny* (1960), p. 69. I have myself conducted many interviews with leading participants in events which I have analysed, for example in *The Inter-American System* (1966).

Lord Acton, the living are far from candid; but so, as I have already stressed, are the dead in what they have written in the documents which form historical evidence. We must not forget that they were alive when they wrote them: that what for us is the past was once the present for those upon whose evidence historians rely in making their reconstruction of past events.

Not only has the contemporary historian a richer variety as well as a greater abundance of materials; by the same token he has also better means of checking upon their reliability. The politician giving an interview or writing his memoirs today is likely to be aware that his interviewer or reviewer is able to check from other sources upon at least a large proportion of his 'facts' and assertions. Contemporary leaders may be no more disinterested than was Julius Caesar when he wrote his *Commentaries*,[1] but the evidence they offer to the contemporary historian is more revealing because so much more easily verified. At the same time, because of the scarcity of other sources, the historian studying Caesar's era has to rely much more heavily upon the *Commentaries* than does the contemporary historian upon comparable material. For recent history, memoirs and diaries – and interviews – are just one class of sources among very many.

Opportunities to conduct interviews and to utilise other such techniques are advantages deriving largely from the circumstance that the contemporary historian really is 'within' the period he is analysing, capturing the feeling of the age – its myths as well as its 'facts' – to an extent which no future historian, however perceptive and painstaking his research, will ever succeed in recapturing. Therefore, a critical analysis of his own times by a trained historian can prove a boon to future historians denied the advantage of having been 'within' them. Thus, in a sense, contemporary historical writing is historically more valuable than are writings of historians concerned with remote periods. Nor must it be forgotten that (as was noted in the first chapter of this book) a great deal of significant history has been contemporary history. It is noteworthy that Thucydides, the Greek historian and one of the founding fathers of the study of history, stressed the great importance of personal experience and observation in striving for knowledge and accuracy. Personal experience and

[1] See above, p. 11.

observation of his own times are essential to every historian, whatever the period of his investigations.[1]

So far in this chapter I have tried to demonstrate that the problems involved in studying contemporary history in the sense of recent or very recent history do not differ fundamentally from those encountered in studying any other period of history; and that the main arguments offered against contemporary history in this sense merely underline weaknesses and contradictions in the professional approach already discussed. As a corollary to this, the study of contemporary history has a special value in correcting these weaknesses. In the first place, it emphasises the nature of history as being concerned with the relationship between present and past, and the essential and indivisible unity of the past, present and future. The contemporary historian, consciously working on the moving frontier of time, is especially aware of changing perspectives and the interim character of judgements. If his field of study encompasses several decades extending to the present day, his research will include working in archives for the earlier parts and analysing the latest serious newspapers and journals – and perhaps interviewing appropriate members of society – for the most recent. Moreover, as he himself matures and gains more experience and expertise, so his judgement develops; while, at the same time, more documentary material becomes available to him in the archives, in the light of which – and of changing perspectives – he constantly is re-examining his earlier conclusions. What is more, the contemporary historian's personal experience of men and events enables him to counter the weakness inherent in the study of history as an examination of documents. For, as Marc Bloch affirmed, 'it is men that history seeks to grasp. Failing that, it will be at best but an exercise in erudition.'[2] One cannot over-stress the point that history is about people and not about documents. It is therefore a salutary experience for any professional historian to do some work in the field of contemporary history. He and his discipline can only benefit from it.

The interpretation which we have been considering hitherto

---

[1] Cf. Galbraith, *An Introduction to the Study of History*, op. cit., p. 18: 'Thucydides, a retired general, wrote an account of the Peloponnesian War (*his* war), which many good judges have held to be the greatest *History* ever written' (Galbraith's italics).
[2] *The Historian's Craft*, op. cit., p. 26.

makes contemporary history merely the most recent period of modern history. Sometimes, however, the attempt is made to distinguish contemporary from modern history not only in terms of time but also in terms of areas of study. In contrast to the Europe-orientated earlier period, contemporary history in this sense is characterised by its concern with 'world history'. The origins of this displacement of Europe may arguably be held to coincide with the opening of the twentieth century. Thus the emergence as world powers of two non-European nations, the United States and Japan, at the end of the nineteenth century, marks one significant starting-point for what might be called the contemporary period.

But contemporary history can be interpreted quite differently. Professor Barraclough, for instance, declares that *'Contemporary history begins when the problems which are actual in the world today first take visible shape'* (his italics).[1] In his judgement, contemporary history follows – or should follow – an almost contrary procedure from 'History of the traditional type' which 'starts at a given point in the past – the French Revolution, for example, or the Industrial Revolution, or the settlement of 1815 – and works systematically forward, tracing a continuous development along lines running forward from the chosen starting-point'.[2] Taking as one illustration the field of international political history from 1815 to the present day, Barraclough maintains that the historian who starts 'from the situation in 1815 and works forward step by step and stage by stage will almost inevitably concern himself mainly with Europe, since the problems which arose directly from the settlement of 1815 were primarily European problems'.[3] On the other hand, 'The historian who takes his stand not in 1815 but in the present will see the same period in different proportions. His starting-point will be the global system of international politics in which we live today and his main concern will be to explain how it arose.'[4] Even so, Barraclough does attempt – not without reservations – to set an approximate date for the beginning of

---

[1] *An Introduction to Contemporary History* (paperback edn., 1967), p. 20.

[2] Ibid., p. 17.

[3] Ibid., p. 18.

[4] Ibid., loc. cit. While Barraclough may not have invented this approach, he has done more than anyone else in this country to draw it to the attention of a wide audience. Cf. Marc Bloch's 'prudently retrogressive method': *The Historian's Craft*, op. cit., pp. 45–6.

contemporary history. 'It is in the years immediately preceding and succeeding 1890', he suggests, 'that most of the developments distinguishing "contemporary" from "modern" history first begin to be visible.'[1]

But the historical analysis of contemporary problems clearly cannot be contained within a particular period. The projection of the analysis will vary with each problem, and with the judgement of the historian. Let me illustrate this point with another passage from Barraclough which deals with a subject of special interest to me. He asks:

> What prospect is there, for example, of assessing realistically the Castro revolution in Cuba if we consider it solely as a manifestation of 'international communism' and fail to relate it either to parallel movements in other parts of the under-developed world or to the long and tangled story of relations between the United States and Cuba since 1901?[2]

Now I would go much further back into the past than Professor Barraclough suggests, for it is my judgement that an understanding of the Cuban revolution calls for an analysis of United States policies in respect of Cuba throughout the nineteenth century. Such an analysis would include an examination of the island's significance in the formulation of the Monroe Doctrine of 1823, for President Monroe was influenced by considerations concerning Cuba's future in making his famous pronouncement against extra-continental intervention in the western hemisphere. That the Monroe Doctrine has never been more seriously challenged than by Cuba's alignment with the Soviet Union in the nineteen-sixties adds a further dimension to the analysis.[3] This challenge has greatly exercised Americans over the last decade. Nearer to home there is, for example, the current problem of Ulster. An historical analysis of the issues involved here would take us back over many centuries.

Both interpretations of contemporary history which we have been discussing have validity as academic enterprises. Some professional historians will be engaged upon the reconstruction of the recent past; they will be contemporary historians in the generally accepted sense of the term. Others may be engaged upon

---

[1] *An Introduction to Contemporary History*, op. cit., p. 24.
[2] Ibid., pp. 15–16.
[3] Connell-Smith, *The Inter-American System*, op. cit., pp. 33–4.

the historical analysis of significant contemporary issues. I have already affirmed my belief that the problems facing the contemporary historian do not differ *fundamentally* from those encountered in conducting research into any other period of history. The contemporary historian needs to master the same basic principles of historical enquiry as his colleagues and, as part of his apprenticeship, to learn to apply them to earlier periods where the materials are more manageable. No less importantly, he must bring to the study of contemporary history a sense of perspective which he may derive from his work on earlier periods. The recent past can be appraised only in the light of the longer perspective, and this applies also – and even more obviously – to the historical analysis of contemporary problems. For these reasons I do not believe that there should be a special category of contemporary historians, trained as such; nor that modern historians should be encouraged slowly to advance the frontier of their research in the manner of modern history examination syllabuses. It is by no means the case that the period of modern history immediately preceding what may be considered the contemporary period is necessarily the most relevant to an understanding of the latter. Nor does the general proposition that what is the most recent in time is necessarily the most relevant – that is to say, has the greatest contemporary significance – have any greater validity.

This equation of 'relevance' with 'contemporary significance' is fundamental to my argument. For what I am advocating in this chapter is not contemporary history as such, but a contemporary approach to history as a discipline based firmly upon its relevance for the intellectual needs of living men: those of the professional historian himself and those of the society of which he is a part (including, of course, his students). In other words, a contemporary approach is 'present-orientated', the study of history being undertaken 'for the present's sake' and 'on the present's terms'. No doubt this will shock those professional historians who believe in eschewing the present in their pursuit of what they deem to be historical truth.

Yet, in a very important sense all historians are contemporary historians. They are quite as much 'men of their time' as the historical figures about whom they write. As I have already stressed, every historian, consciously or unconsciously, brings to

his understanding of the past the experience of his own generation; and each generation sees the past differently from the way
in which its predecessors saw it. Professional historians tend to
stress the importance of fresh documents and new techniques in
the process of refining historical judgements. But the great
stimulant of new questions and new insights regarding our
appreciation of historical situations is the changing experience of
society itself. On this last point, for example, Professor E. J.
Hobsbawm observes in respect of a significant aspect of the
French revolution:

> In the course of its crisis the young French Republic dis-
> covered or invented total war . . . How appalling the implica-
> tions of this discovery are has only become clear in our own
> historic epoch. Since the revolutionary war of 1792–4
> remained an exceptional episode, most nineteenth-century
> observers could make no sense of it . . . Only today can we
> see how much about the Jacobin Republic and the 'Terror'
> of 1793–4 makes sense in no other terms than those of a
> modern total war effort.[1]

In more general terms, experience of the Russian revolution has
greatly enhanced the historian's understanding of the French
revolution. No historian, however hard he may mistakenly try to
divorce his reconstruction of the past from his experience of the
present, can succeed in doing so. What he can do, unfortunately,
is to limit the contribution to his work of his own personal
experience, and thus reduce an important element in his interpretation of the past.[2] For no amount of technical expertise can
compensate for the lack of knowledge of life. While such expertise
will increase the historian's competence in establishing what a
document says, it will not enable him to assess the motives of the
man who wrote it.[3] In the previous chapter I commented upon
the serious weakness inherent in the tendency of professional
historians to undertake research into subjects which are remote

---

[1] *The Age of Revolution, 1789–1848* (paperback edn., 1962), p. 90.

[2] Professor Elton tells us, for example (*Political History: Principles and Practice*,
op. cit., p. 54, n. 5): 'I know myself that a year spent in political police work after
World War II (in about as humble capacity as can be imagined) has given me
permanent enlightenment about some of the essential realities of any society which
no amount of imaginative groping could have taught as well.'

[3] Cf. L. B. Namier, *Avenues of History* (1952), p. 4: 'study unsupported by practical
experience will seldom produce a historian: hence the poverty of a great deal of
history written by cloistered generations.'

from their present interests and experience.[1] A contemporary approach predicates active recognition by the historian of his own place in time and that of contemporary society; and active awareness of the continual change which he and society are undergoing. It is an approach which seeks not the static 'what really happened' but the dynamic, because ever changing, contemporary significance of historical phenomena.

✗ A contemporary approach does not attempt to establish what really happened *as an end in itself*. Above all, it rejects the emphasis placed upon the particular character of historical events and the fragmentation of history to which it leads. In a contemporary approach, the historian does endeavour in the formulation of his judgement to analyse an historical situation within its own context. But his over-riding concern is to assess its significance in the light of changing human experience. A contemporary approach emphasises that historical understanding demands the widest range of comparison between different but related situations. Thus it opposes undue specialisation which promotes learning at the expense of understanding; and stresses the need for the professional historian to link his field of specialised research with wider fields and to comparable (though necessarily different) situations perhaps remote from it in time.

I have already criticised what I consider to be the undue preoccupation of professional historians with documents: a preoccupation which emphasises means at the expense of ends. Clearly it is essential to determine, with the greatest possible accuracy, what a document says, to establish its authenticity and so on. Thus we need the techniques which historians have developed for such purposes as exposing forgeries, authenticating texts and validating dates. But palaeography, diplomatic and other such skills are merely auxiliary to the discipline of history. Let us refer once more to one of the most famous of all historical documents: Magna Carta.[2] The Great Charter is, of course, written in medieval Latin, and there has been considerable debate over the exact meaning of certain parts of it. What is involved basically is the question of how far Magna Carta was merely a treaty concerned with the privileges of the barons who forced its acceptance upon King John, or a document concerned with

[1] See above, p. 45.
[2] See above, p. 62.

safeguarding English liberties: in other words, the debate is over the meaning of Magna Carta to those who wrote it. I do not wish to denigrate the scholarly work of those who have attempted to resolve this problem. But I do assert that what should be vastly more important for historians is the changing significance of Magna Carta through time: the interpretations made of it by John's immediate successors (and their opponents) and by later generations of politicians and lawyers in England and North America – to mention a fraction of those whose lives have been affected by what the Great Charter was believed to have established. Magna Carta had little enough significance for most of the people who were alive when it was signed; it has had much greater significance in the subsequent political and constitutional history of England and of the United States.

Another document to which I referred earlier also illustrates the point I am making, although it does not present a comparable problem of textual interpretation: the Monroe Doctrine.[1] President Monroe's Message is much more significant for what it has come to mean for successive generations of Americans[2] and in different historical situations than for what Monroe actually said on 2 December, 1823. Of course the historian is concerned to know what these documents say, and as much as possible about the circumstances in which they came to be written. But these matters should form only a part – and by no means necessarily the most important part – of their significance for him. Indeed, in the cases of Magna Carta and the Monroe Doctrine it is precisely their subsequent significance that has given them such interest for historians. Perhaps an even better example of 'subsequent significance' is furnished by the English parliament, whose overwhelming prominence in historical writings on the English constitution hardly derives from the actual achievement of the knights of the shires and the burgesses of the towns called upon to attend its early meetings.

Significance through time, then, is an essential feature of a contemporary approach to the study of history. That approach is importantly linked with the question of selection now that the

---

[1] See above, p. 72. What is known as 'The Original Monroe Doctrine' consists of two passages in the Message. See Dexter Perkins, *A History of the Monroe Doctrine* (1960), pp. 394–6.

[2] In both the United States and Latin America.

vast amount of material available to historians has created a situation totally different from the one upon which the professional approach is predicated. As has been shown on numerous occasions in this book, there is nothing new in the idea of contemporary significance – or relevance. I made the point in the previous chapter that the emphasis hitherto placed upon English constitutional history, for example, derives from its relevance at a time when the world (and, above all, Britain's place in it) was very different from what it is today. The relatively great increase in the study of African, Asian and Latin American history, and the establishment of new centres and schools to further studies in these areas, reflect recognition of great changes which have taken place in the world. They are altogether healthy developments. We need greater knowledge of these areas, and must encourage scholars to enlighten us (*and not just one another*) about them.

These new institutions perform two particularly useful functions. First of all, they are inter-disciplinary, bringing together historians and other scholars with special interests in the areas concerned. Secondly, they increase contacts between scholars and interested laymen. For example, in his review of the progress made in the development of Latin American studies in this country following the Parry Report,[1] the Secretary of the Institute of Latin American Studies in London observed:

Another aspect of the growth of Latin American studies in Great Britain which requires emphasis in coming years is the need for those in universities to go outside the walls. The support given to the Parry Committee by the business community was one of the factors in its success, and the connection has been maintained, in part, by an annual course organised at the London Institute, specifically for businessmen and staff of government departments on some particular region of Latin America. These courses benefit the academic world no less than that of commerce . . . for the academic, the confrontation of his (usually) more detached and wider vision with the day-to-day reality can be . . . refreshing.[2]

[1] *Report of the Committee on Latin American Studies* (1965). The Report is usually referred to as the Parry Report, after the Chairman of the Committee, Dr. J. H. Parry.

[2] Harold Blakemore, *Latin American Studies in British Universities: Progress and Prospects* (1971), p. 22.

One hopes that these extra-mural activities will indeed be emphasised. Another, though different, kind of institution which brings scholars (especially those interested in contemporary history) and laymen together for their common advantage is the Royal Institute of International Affairs. An unofficial body, founded in 1920 'to encourage and facilitate the scientific study of international questions', this Institute fulfils its purposes through:

> the organization of research into international problems by individual scholars and by study groups composed of experts and others representing diverse points of view; the publication of books, periodicals and pamphlets; the arrangement of lectures and discussions on matters of current interest; and the maintenance of a specialised library of books and documents on international affairs, together with a library of classified press information drawn from a wide international selection of newspapers.[1]

The Royal Institute of International Affairs is an important meeting place for scholars of different disciplines together with educated laymen concerned with significant contemporary issues.

In the previous chapter I asserted that society may reasonably expect two main things from the professional historian, in addition to his function as a university teacher: satisfaction of its curiosity about the past, and some guidance on present issues and problems. I made little comment on the second of these, and would like to say more now. The reluctance of so many professional historians to write on general themes for educated laymen – and suspicion of those of their colleagues who do so – is paralleled by their denial of any special competence to offer guidance on contemporary issues. This denial, which tallies with their attitude towards contemporary history, is related also to their insistence upon the particular character of historical events and their attempt to divorce the past from the present. It also contains a strong element of intellectual snobbery, evident in their scornful rejection of the notion that the study of history should be 'useful'. Their grounds for such a rejection seem to be that the only alternative to it is acceptance of the idea that the past furnishes 'a key to current problems, a series of patterns which we can immediately transpose into the context of contemporary

[1] Royal Institute of International Affairs, *Annual Report of the Council, 1969–70*, p. 2.

politics'.[1] This is a preposterous idea. No responsible historian would subscribe to it. And teachers of history hardly need to be told that they 'must set their faces against the necessarily ignorant demands of "society" . . . for immediate applicability'.[2]

Leaving aside such extravagances, what may society reasonably expect from professional historians in the way of guidance on current issues and problems? In the first place, since they claim that history is concerned with all aspects of human experience, society can reasonably expect to draw upon that experience when faced with serious problems. It will be interested to know how human beings acted in relevant situations in the past and what were the consequences of their actions. And surely not even the most adamant opponent of the idea of history's providing 'lessons' would deny that knowledge of the historical background to a problem helps us to understand it; and that understanding is a prerequisite to finding a solution. But very many historians would agree with Professor Elton when he says:

> that the 'usefulness' of historical studies lies hardly at all in the knowledge they purvey and in the understanding of specific present problems from their prehistory; it lies much more in the fact that they produce standards of judgement and powers of reasoning which they alone develop, which arise from their very essence, and which are unusually clear-headed, balanced and compassionate.[3]

I agree, *in principle*, with Elton's main point. The development of 'standards of judgement and powers of reasoning' *should be* the most important contribution of historical studies to a person's education; though – as I have made clear – I set much greater store than does Elton by their value in increasing knowledge and understanding of the world we live in. But I have also made clear my very considerable doubts about the extent to which, *in practice*, the professional approach to the study of history does produce such standards and powers. I see overmuch pedantry and narrowness of vision – as well as confusion over the nature and purposes of their discipline – among professional historians. But, if historical studies really do possess unique qualities, does

---

[1] Geoffrey Barraclough, *History in a Changing World* (1955), p. 184. Of course, Professor Barraclough is no subscriber to such an idea.
[2] G. R. Elton, 'Second Thoughts on History at the Universities', *History*, vol. liv (1969), p. 66.
[3] Ibid., loc. cit.

not this increase the professional historian's obligation to society, especially at a time of such doubt and questioning of our institutions and values? And in an age of rapid, disconcerting change, should not a discipline claiming to be uniquely concerned with the changing circumstances of human society have a vital contribution to make to an understanding of our present problems?

Clearly, the professional approach precludes such a contribution: it renders historians both unwilling and unable to make it. A contemporary approach, on the other hand, recognises the historian's obligation – and opportunity – in this regard, and develops his competence to discharge it. It recognises that history is not basically a technical subject, and cannot be contained within the walls of muniment rooms and university departments; nor confined between the covers of learned books and professional journals. History has long been established in the political arena, as Lloyd illustrated in the first chapter. It may have ceased to be 'past politics', but present politics have a strong historical content. A distinguished historian reminds us of 'the historical assumptions which are implicit in most language and in all political judgements'.[1] The same historian refers to journalists, aptly in my opinion, as 'the historians who write for the daily newspaper'.[2] Politicians are very conscious of history, and seek to use it as well as to make it. Dr. Fidel Castro, the Cuban leader, is but one in a long line of politicians who have declared, in effect, 'History will absolve me'.[3] Others aspire to write 'instant' history soon after leaving office, and very revealing documents their writings are proving to be.

I have already referred to the use made of Magna Carta over the centuries to serve political purposes. Do we need to be reminded that the Great Charter was written originally to serve such purposes, and not those of historical research? A recent biographer of William the Conqueror – to take a perhaps less obvious example – has asserted that 'For generations he has remained, so to speak, a figure in contemporary politics'.[4] It may

[1] G. Kitson Clark, *The Critical Historian* (1967), p. 8.

[2] Ibid., p. 12.

[3] This is the title of the widely published version of Dr. Castro's defence speech at his trial in 1953 for his part in the unsuccessful raid on the Moncada Barracks in Santiago de Cuba. It has become a major document of the Cuban revolution.

[4] David C. Douglas, *William the Conqueror: The Norman Impact upon England* (paperback edn., 1969), p. 5.

not, indeed, be too fanciful to suggest that the establishment of the Anglo-Norman kingdom in the eleventh century has some relevance to the present, but clearly (as the politicians have been so assiduous in reminding us) historic, issue of Britain's joining the European Economic Community. Historical analogies are continually being drawn, with varying degrees of validity. In the years immediately after the Second World War the policy of rearmament against a possible threat from the Soviet Union to British security was justified by reference to the failure of the policy of appeasement in the immediate pre-war years.[1] More specifically, Sir Anthony Eden drew a parallel between Gamal Abdul Nasser and Adolf Hitler in justifying the policy of armed intervention in Egypt in 1956.[2] Politicians often are importantly influenced by their reading of history. Hitler's addiction to Thomas Carlyle's *History of Frederick the Great* is well known[3]; the Bolshevik leaders were much preoccupied with possible lessons to be drawn from the French revolution – apparently with significant influence upon the respective fortunes of Stalin and Trotsky.[4]

What happened in the past has helped to shape man's present environment; what he thinks happened does have influence upon his present and future actions. Thus history embraces both 'facts' and myths; it engages both professionals and laymen. It is not, therefore, a question of whether historians should take their subject into the market place and the pulpit – or rather into the newspapers and on to the television screens. History is already there. Never before have ordinary men and women been so aware of the great issues which affect them so nearly nor more in need of guidance in forming their judgements upon them. Never before has there been a greater need for historical judgement. Yet so many historians withdraw from society, protesting that

[1] On the other hand, some historians have drawn an analogy between the 'Cold War' and the religious wars of the sixteenth and seventeenth centuries, e.g. Bullock, op. cit., p. 70; A. J. P. Taylor, *Europe: Grandeur and Decline* (1967), p. 369.

[2] Sir Anthony Eden, *Memoirs: Full Circle* (1960), pp. 431-2, etc. The analogy between Nasser and Hitler – and Mussolini – was made by politicians of both main parties at the time. See, for example, Harold Macmillan, *Riding the Storm, 1956-1959* (1971), pp. 102, 131, 148.

[3] See, for example, H. R. Trevor-Roper, *The Last Days of Hitler* (paperback edn., 1962), pp. 140, 260.

[4] See, for example, Isaac Deutscher, *Stalin: A Political Biography* (paperback edn., 1966), pp. 275, etc.

their discipline has no relevance to its problems. This is not only an abdication of responsibility. It is an invitation to others to discharge the historian's proper function in other – ultimately less valuable – ways.

As I indicated in the previous chapter, the professional historian's inclination to withdraw from present society and its problems has particularly serious implications for his most important social function: that of teacher. I want now, therefore, to consider the application of a contemporary approach to that function. I have already emphasised that such an approach to history as a discipline is based firmly upon its relevance to the intellectual needs of living men, and thus of students who read the subject at university. Now – as we have reminded readers – the aim of university education, of which history forms a part, is to equip men and women for their lives in the world. The study of history can make a special contribution to the fulfilment of this broad aim by helping students to develop judgement through analysing the changing circumstances of human society, and to increase their knowledge and understanding of the world they live in. These two aspects of history's role in university education I regard as essentially complementary, and certainly in no sensible way antagonistic to each other. Neither purpose will be served by students attempting to study the past 'for its own sake': through their being encouraged to adopt the professional approach to the practice of history as I have described it. Both will be furthered by an approach which acknowledges the relevance of history and seeks to establish a meaningful relationship between present and past situations, thus enabling men and women to derive the maximum benefit from the vast store of human experience.

Since, as a teacher, the professional historian has to draw upon as well as to broaden the experience of his students, it is important for him purposefully to bring together the present, in which his students' experience largely lies, and the past, which they are trying to understand. It is not so much a question of drawing parallels as of recognising differences – and so of appreciating change; and this cannot be done merely by focussing upon the particular in the past. Let us consider, for example, a student who is attempting to comprehend the issue of frontiers in European diplomacy in the seventeenth century. He requires first a general idea of what the term 'frontier' signifies. Next, he must guard against a gratuitous equation of contemporary frontier issues with comparable issues in the seventeenth century. By grasping the difference, he gains insight into the all-important historical consideration of change.[1] He also becomes better able to understand the seventeenth-century circumstances with which for the moment he is concerned. Constant comparison between the present and the past (and between different parts of the past – never forgetting that what we call 'the present' is for the historian the most recent part of the past) is vital in developing the history student's judgement upon men and events.

Professional historians continually stress the danger of reading 'present attitudes' into the past, and are correspondingly anxious to try to divorce the past from the present in order to avoid falling into this 'cardinal error'. On the other hand, my own experience of students suggests that only too often they are less in danger of reading the present into the past than of possessing too little awareness and knowledge of the present to be able to establish a meaningful relationship between it and the past. They tend to immerse themselves in books on historical subjects without attempting to utilise their present experience to formulate the kind of questions they should ask in relation to these subjects, and to distinguish the types of information they should seek in order to obtain the answers. Only too many history students discuss institutions, and use terms, of whose present meaning and changing significance they have only the haziest conception. Under these circumstances, meaningful analysis of historical events and of people involved in them is not possible. Students go off to their libraries to accumulate information about, let us say, Sweden's role in seventeenth-century Europe, without pausing to ask themselves why Sweden does not play a comparable role today; in what ways Europe in the seventeenth century differed from Europe today (and, indeed, from Europe in the sixteenth and eighteenth centuries); and such other questions relating to changing patterns of power and international relations which might stimulate ideas. So many busy themselves with the mindless recording of what they deem to be facts, uncritically copied from books and learned articles recommended by their tutors, without reference to real situations and real people.

[1] See below, p. 106.

Regrettably, the professional approach is well calculated to encourage this kind of sterile endeavour. It must be abandoned.

In this chapter I have been concerned with formulating a contemporary approach to the practice of history, harmonising the historian's roles as scholar, citizen and teacher. I have devoted a good proportion of the chapter to an examination of the nature of contemporary history, and the objections of many professional historians to it. Antipathy towards contemporary history is linked with a comparable attitude towards relevance, and has the same roots in the professional approach. Contemporary historians have tended to be on the defensive in meeting criticisms that their studies are not 'real' history nor truly 'scholarly'. Such diffidence – as I have indicated – is quite uncalled for. An analysis of the objections to contemporary history inherent in the professional approach confirms the latter's fundamental contradictions and, indeed, reveals further weaknesses. For this reason I believe that the study of contemporary history furnishes an urgently needed corrective to the professional approach, and that a shift of emphasis towards contemporary history is vital for the future of the discipline.

In addition to underlining its inherent contradictions, contemporary history confirms the breakdown of the professional approach which occurred long ago. As we have seen, the professional approach predicates there being a limited amount of surviving material. Historical knowledge could, under such circumstances, be regarded as finite and therefore the possibility of establishing what happened in the knowable past seriously entertained by scholars. Confronted by the masses of documents available for reconstructing the recent past, the contemporary historian is forced to recognise that, for all practical purposes, the amount of historical knowledge is infinite. In this situation, the historian who clings to the now quite irrelevant professional approach can only take refuge in the claim that recent history is not real history at all. But, in that case, what can he reply if pressed to declare when, in his view, real history ended? An equation of history with 'the past' – which such an historian is inclined to make – adds to his embarrassment, since yesterday is as surely the past as a thousand years ago.

In short, contemporary history performs an extremely valuable service to the discipline in highlighting delusions to which professional historians are so prone. The contemporary historian cannot, in the first place, entertain the notion that it is possible to eliminate himself and his present circumstances from his pursuit of historical understanding. He is always aware – as all historians should be – of his own place in time and in the continuous and changing process of history.[1] He can be under no illusion about the possibility of divorcing 'the past' from 'the present'; nor can he for a moment believe this to be desirable even were it attainable. The contemporary historian cannot believe that what he is doing will one day form part of a universal, definitive history. He knows only too well that the proportion of the knowable past which the historian can establish is a minute and rapidly diminishing one. His task is to assess the significance of such historical phenomena as come within the scope of his studies; for him, the mere compilation of 'facts' can only be the futile enterprise which, in truth, it is for any historian. For him, judgement in selecting his materials and in assessing their significance has relegated technical expertise to the tool it properly is; formulating the relevant questions has superseded the establishment of 'what happened'. He knows what being 'within' a period really means. He knows the value of personal experience in a world of real people and not one created by imaginative groping in which such experience is an unwelcome albeit persistent intruder.

Thus, in my judgement, the study of recent history, in underlining the contradictions and delusions inherent in the professional approach, points the way to a contemporary approach to the practice of history. Such an approach is 'contemporary' above all in its relevance to the present, rapidly changing circumstances of our discipline, of the institutions in which it is practised, and of society at large. A contemporary approach elevates the practical needs of living people above theoretical obligations to 'the past' and to 'posterity' – or even to that most elusive of concepts, 'objective truth'. It rejects as mere antiquarianism the compilation of facts about the past regardless of their relevance to wider

[1] Cf. Professor E. H. Carr's apt comments on the likening of history to a 'moving procession' (*What is History?*, paperback edn., 1964, pp. 35–36): 'The metaphor is fair enough, provided it does not tempt the historian to think of himself as an eagle surveying the scene from a lonely crag or as a V.I.P. at the saluting base. Nothing of the kind! The historian is just another dim figure trudging along in another part of the procession.'

purposes having contemporary significance. Relevance and the contemporary – and thus changing – significance of historical phenomena are the essential characteristics of a contemporary approach, *however remote those phenomena may be in time*. A contemporary approach stresses the concern of history with change in human society and with the totality of human experience. It therefore condemns the fragmentation of history and that emphasis upon autonomy which shuns cooperation with other disciplines in the search for 'truth' about 'the past'. In the advancement of historical scholarship, a contemporary approach values the development of judgement above the mere employment of technical expertise.

A contemporary approach likewise stresses the social functions of history. It emphasises the involvement of the professional historian in society, and the importance of his addressing himself to educated laymen and not just to other professionals. It rejects the extraordinary notion that 'real' history consists of those displays of expertise on recondite topics which professional historians put on to impress each other. It rejects as no less extraordinary the notion that somehow society *needs* and benefits from this kind of activity. The products of such activity languish between the covers of learned books and periodicals. Either they never reach the attention of laymen in any form; or if they do reach laymen through the medium of general works, they cease to be 'real' history in professional eyes. A contemporary approach dismisses all this as preposterous. It accepts the involvement of the historian in society as essential to the effective practice of the discipline itself, quite apart from the performance of its important social functions. A professional historian who has not a lively interest in his own time is a poorer scholar, because personal experience is a vital element in developing judgement of men and affairs. At the same time, a contemporary approach predicates a constant awareness by the historian of the relevance of what he is doing for the society of which he is a member: an awareness of himself as a citizen and the obligations which stem from this fact.

This brings me, finally, to the most important aspect of the historian's approach to his subject: his role as an educator. He performs this role in some measure by addressing himself to laymen, to whom he should give some guidance and instruction – as well as pleasure. But the professional historian has the specific task, entrusted to him by society, of contributing to the education of its young people. A contemporary approach recognises the imperative need for the study of history to be directly relevant to this purpose. I have shown some of the harmful consequences of projecting the professional approach into the teaching of history to university students and to pupils in our schools; and have indicated some advantages of adopting a contemporary approach. But the mere projection of a contemporary approach into the teaching of history is not enough. For history to be an effective medium of education – its main social function – requires the application of sound educational principles appropriate to it, of which most professional historians are woefully ignorant. A searching examination of these principles in relation to our discipline is conducted by Lloyd in the chapter which follows.

4 History and Education

In the first chapter of this book I explained the continued practice of history from Herodotus to the nineteenth century in terms of its relevance both to current circumstances in the eyes of contemporaries and as a medium of instruction. In the mid-nineteenth century the subject became established in English universities owing specifically to its presumed relevance as an educational medium. Such a view was held both by those who thought the purpose of education to be bound up with considerations of public utility, and by those who thought its purpose to be improvement of the powers of the individual mind. History has since been widely taught not only in universities but also in schools, where educational medicine has been extensively mixed to university prescriptions.

Meanwhile historians have been preoccupied with pursuing learning and cultivating scholarship by means of the professional approach, which Connell-Smith has analysed. For the sake of 'the past' they have set their faces against relevance, and have cultivated quasi-scientific study of documents surviving from the remote past and illustrative of particular events above historical analysis of broad issues possessing contemporary significance. Connell-Smith has argued on practical grounds that this approach is invalid. Moreover, it constitutes on the part of historians an abdication of responsibility that is detrimental to the future place of history within the educational system and within society. In its place he has advocated an approach whereby the historian exercises his judgement upon historical phenomena, whether they be remote or recent in time, by reference to their significance for contemporaries. Such an historian addresses himself specifically to his fellow-citizens and to his pupils, and so demonstrates for their benefit, and not merely for his own or his fellow-professionals', the relevance of history.

As we recognised at the outset, arguments for relevance

presented in practical terms are uncongenial to the academic mind, of which the professional historian's is an excellent example. Academics find it more congenial to regard their role as the pursuit of learning, an activity which they interpret less in a practical than in a metaphysical sense. They cherish an ideal where the pursuer of learning is absorbed into the object of his pursuit. It is with such an end in view that the professional historian endeavours to abandon 'the present', to enter into 'the past' and to see it 'from within', 'on its own terms'. Even when academics accept that they have an educational function to discharge and describe themselves accordingly, ideal considerations remain paramount. As the historian of the Association of University Teachers has remarked:[1]

> To most university teachers the highest academic responsibility is neither to the students nor to society, important as they are, but to the subject itself, and in the final analysis to truth, or, if that is too absolute and abstract a concept in a relativistic age, to mankind's total stock of objective knowledge.

But ideals have to survive, if at all, in a practical and changing world; and the world of academics has undergone rapid change during the last decade. In the wake of the Robbins Commission report the universities have expanded very rapidly, have taken on the task of teaching increasing numbers of students, have received and spent large sums of money provided by society, have acquired buildings, libraries and equipment on a lavish scale, and have not been backward in asking for more. These developments have occurred in the name of higher education. Certainly the universities have retained within the country's educational system a degree of independence and self-government that is the envy of less favoured institutions. Yet their practical involvement with that system and with society has obviously become much greater than before. So pressures have grown upon academics to account for their activities in practical terms, and to declare their educational aims.

The Robbins Commissioners identified four aims for higher education.[2] One of these, 'the advancement of learning', was

[1] H. Perkin, *Key Profession: The History of the Association of University Teachers* (1969), p. 246.
[2] Committee on Higher Education, *Report of the Committee appointed by the Prime Minister under the Chairmanship of Lord Robbins, 1961–3* (1963), pp. 6–7.

acceptable enough in academic circles. A second, expressed as 'the transmission of a common culture', was too vaguely defined to constitute a challenge to academic attitudes. The third aim – significantly, placed first in order by the Commissioners – was more explicit, and less acceptable as their choice of words implied: 'there is no betrayal of values when institutions of higher education teach what will be of some practical use'. This contention has had different implications for practitioners of different academic disciplines. Practitioners of the natural and social sciences have had no difficulty in claiming practical relevance for what they do; and since what they do is generally couched in terminology beyond the understanding of laymen, the claim is largely immune to challenge by the uninitiated. Indeed, some such practitioners, most notably economists like Lord Robbins himself, have capitalised heavily on the developments of the last decade and have lost no opportunity of publicly tossing concepts and quantities back and forth to the bewilderment of the lay bystander though greatly – as they assure him – to his advantage. Practitioners of the modern European languages have for the usefulness of their discipline no less self-evident a case, which has gained further impact as England has sidled closer to Europe. But for historians, determined to distinguish themselves from social scientists, less well protected by jargon despite their earnest endeavours, and driven along the professional approach to divorce their 'past' from the present, the old argument for history's public utility has lost its serviceability.

However, the Robbins Commissioners also identified another aim for higher education: that 'what is taught should be taught in such a way as to promote the general powers of the mind'. This harmonised with the other long-standing argument for history as an educational medium. It is in such terms as these that professional historians have made their educational case for their discipline. The case has been stated most emphatically by Professor Elton:

> Three or four years spent at a university cannot teach a man to know history . . . But if those years do not produce an effective conditioning of the reasoning mind, if they do not teach a man to think better than otherwise he would have done, they may justly be condemned as a waste of time.[1]

[1] *The Practice of History*, op. cit., p. 186.

To this extent professional historians have conceded that history does have relevance. It is a hazardous concession. While many other academics may defend the educational validity of their disciplines merely by reference to the utility of the subject-matter involved, it seems that historians must defend theirs by reference to its effects upon the minds of those who study it. For staunch believers in history 'for its own sake', the position is surely an embarrassment. It is the more embarrassing since historians are normally no better equipped than other academics in matters of educational psychology.

Like other university teachers, every professional historian owes his appointment to his proven ability as a scholar in some field of research. Once appointed, he finds that although he is required to teach as well as to carry out research, his prospects of future promotion depend principally upon his continuing to furnish proof of ability and zeal in the latter. Such proof takes the form of publications, in scholarly periodicals or by reputable publishing-houses: evidence visible to his fellow-scholars of the academic's devotion to the pursuit of learning. For the historian preparation of such evidence is a time-consuming business. It may involve him in learning new languages and new techniques. It certainly involves him in painstaking searches through books and archives for relevant information; in long hours of reflection upon the material he has gathered; in gradual refinement of initial judgements, and ultimately in arduous processes of composition. No more than his fellow-academics does he have time to spare for studying educational theory and practice. And so, like them, he relies as a teacher upon what he knows as a scholar. This governs the way in which he sets about his teaching.

In this chapter I will identify two educational approaches. I will comment upon their respective suitability for history-teaching, and will show how the historian's current reliance upon the first constitutes a further indictment of the professional approach. Dimly aware that their educational performance is unsatisfactory, historians have made some attempt to improve it. But a fundamental alteration of approach is necessary if the educational case for history is to be sustained and the subject's place safeguarded within educational institutions at every level. History is vulnerable at the present time, and the chief responsibility both for its current predicament and for its future prospects rests with its university teachers, the professional historians. If their claim that historical study improves the powers of the mind is to be vindicated, they will have to abandon the professional approach and apply themselves, along lines which I will attempt to outline, far more seriously and far more concertedly to their educational task than presently they do.

Every educational situation may be expressed as a triangle having as its points a teacher, a pupil, and information relating to a field of study. There are in principle two alternative approaches for the teacher, and these are discernible in the history of education. In practice the distinction between them is far from absolute, but nonetheless obtains in terms of emphasis and priorities. The first is the information-orientated approach. By this approach the chief emphasis falls upon matters, such as facts, and upon procedures, such as techniques of analysis, which are generally accepted as correct. Together these constitute information, and the teacher's role is essentially one of communicating information to his pupils. For him, questions of syllabus, or the information-content of courses of study, are very important. He begins by deciding upon this content, and takes his decisions by reference to criteria derived from the entire body of information available to him. Having done so, he favours teaching-methods which allow the information he has chosen to be communicated to all his pupils, since it is important that they hear what he has to tell them. He also favours methods which allow the pupils in their turn to demonstrate their familiarity with the stipulated area of information. Perhaps the finest example of this approach in practice is the rigorous, and also highly centralised, system of education evolved in France in the course of the nineteenth century, notably under the direction of F. P. G. Guizot, Minister of Public Instruction and sometime Professor of History in the University of Paris.[1]

In schools and universities alike, the main teaching-methods consistent with the information-orientated approach are those of lecture and examination. By 'lecture' I mean any teaching-situation, whether it is formally so described or whether it has the less formal appearance of a seminar, which consists of an extended monologue by the teacher to pupils who, as the 1964 Hale Committee expressed it, 'have nothing to do except to listen and

[1] For a critical account of Guizot as an educationist, see D. Johnson, *Guizot* (1963), pp. 88–154.

take notes'.[1] By 'examination' I mean any situation where pupils are required to present within a limited amount of time answers to briefly-stated questions concerning their field of study in order that their performance may be assessed in terms of literal or numerical marks. In the light of Connell-Smith's analysis of the nature of historical study, these methods have obvious disadvantages for history-teaching. Members of lecture-audiences very readily accept as sufficient and correct the lecturer's summation of the current state of historical information concerning the topic of his lecture. They all too readily fail to recognise the subjective nature of historical interpretation, and overlook that the discipline's essential concern is with making judgements which are always interim upon situations which are always changing. When lectures are followed by examinations, the disadvantages multiply. Now the pupil has to think rapidly and record his answers at speed. It is Professor Elton who has warned us against 'a theory that a ready ability to write comes only to the historian equipped with full knowledge. One could wish it were so, but in fact only ignorance makes the writing of history easy.'[2] Surely the historian as teacher ought to be steadfast against ignorance. In short, that painstaking, reflective and ultimately subjective process that in our judgement constitutes historical study is severely distorted and caricatured by the methods of the information-orientated approach.

Of course, observations of this kind are nothing new. Just as eminent historians have issued warnings against 'professionalism',[3] so have eminent historians commented on the disadvantages to history inherent in information-orientated methods, and have proposed alternatives. Nearly thirty years ago, Sir Maurice Powicke stressed the limitations of 'formal instruction in class' in teaching history, and the desirability of taking history-teaching 'very leisurely', of having 'small groups for discussion', of giving the pupil 'opportunities for the exercise of the historical judgement', and of having 'no examinations, in the usual sense of the term, of any kind'.[4] Half a century has passed since T. F. Tout introduced the long essay, or 'thesis', as a part of assessment for

---

[1] University Grants Committee, *Report of the Committee on University Teaching Methods* (1964), Appendix VII, Part ii (1).
[2] *The Practice of History*, op. cit., p. 115.
[3] See above, p. 47.
[4] F. M. Powicke, *Modern Historians and the Study of History* (1955), pp. 231–2.

final honours in history at Manchester. Such recognition of education as a gradual process requiring active involvement on the part of pupils and dealings between them as well as with the teacher, is characteristic of the second educational approach. It is the pupil-orientated approach which, in terms of emphasis and priorities, is fundamentally different from that which bears primarily upon information.

By the pupil-orientated approach the chief emphasis falls upon the pupil's realisation of himself and his abilities. The teacher's role is essentially one of observing and guiding every pupil according to his individual capacities and needs. Such a teacher discounts formalised questions of syllabus and standard imperatives of information, for these ought not to be permitted arbitrarily to dictate the pupil's development. He favours teaching-methods where the pupil is placed in a situation that excites his interest, and is stimulated to discern problems and to set about solving them on his own account. The pupil does so by himself seeking out information at his own pace, by comparing his ideas with those of other pupils, as well as by consulting with his teacher. Such an approach has been advocated by a long line of educational thinkers. Prominent among them in the twentieth century have been the philosophers John Dewey and Bertrand Russell, strongly in agreement on educational matters despite their philosophical differences. Among their forerunners in the nineteenth century was Friedrich Froebel, founder of the first Kindergarten. Earlier still, in the sixteenth century the French essayist Montaigne condemned modes of education whereby 'The usual way is to bawl into a pupil's ears as if one were pouring water into a funnel, and the boy's business is simply to repeat what he is told. I would have the tutor amend this state of things', he added, 'and begin straight away to exercise the mind that he is training, according to its capacities.'[1]

In general, such thinkers have been chiefly concerned with the education of young children. In our own time, the pupil-orientated approach has gained much ground at the level of the primary school. It is also apparent in the way in which university postgraduate students have traditionally been taught. At secon-

[1] See J. Dewey, *Democracy and Education* (1915); B. Russell, *History of Western Philosophy* (2nd edn., 1961), p. 774; F. Froebel, *The Education of Man* (1826); Michel de Montaigne, *Essays*, trans. J. M. Cohen (1958), p. 54.

dary school and undergraduate levels the main teaching-methods consistent with it are those of the individual tutorial linked with the small discussion-group and with the preparation by each pupil, over extended periods of time, of lengthy projects, essays or dissertations. For history-teaching these methods have advantages that would be obvious, were it not for the professional approach. When the pupil is actively engaged in discerning problems and solving them according to his own judgement, he is surely emulating the way in which an historian sets about his work. As he reads for himself different interpretations written at different times of comparable historical situations and then attempts to formulate an interpretation of his own, he is less likely than in the lecture to be deceived by appearances of certainty and to overlook considerations of change. Gradual refinement of judgement in the light of additional information and alternative views is promoted by discussion and by protracted exercises in composition under tutorial supervision. The practice fostered by examinations of summary and rapid answers to brief questions upon disconnected topics finds no place in the pupil-orientated approach.

These principles are plain enough. They would seem accessible to every historian simply by reference to his own experience. Yet lectures and examinations, the methods consistent with the information-orientated approach, have been and continue to be extremely prominent in history-teaching, from the level of the secondary school to university graduation. Indeed, such methods are invading postgraduate teaching, where one-year lecture-courses culminating in examinations and a higher degree are annually becoming more numerous. Of course, these methods are not peculiar to history-teaching. One plausible explanation for reluctance to abandon the information-orientated approach at any level of education and in any type of discipline lies in controversy amongst psychologists over the way in which intelligence develops in pupils of every age, and thus debate over the methods most appropriate to fostering their abilities. We will return to this question in due course; it is an important matter for historians and their claim that historical study improves mental powers. But it is not upon such grounds as these that professional historians may account for their extensive use of information-orientated methods in their teaching. Since few of them possess any expertise in educational psychology, they cannot normally evaluate their educational approach in psychological terms. However, they may advance a number of other arguments for their reliance upon lectures and examinations. But these arguments reflect very badly upon professional history.

In general, the main argument for information-orientated methods is that the information communicated by the teacher to the pupil is of practical use to him and will remain so. As we have seen, historians make no such claim for history. But from this main argument there may be derived two more, each involving the nature and form of the information in question. The first is that the information communicated to pupils in lectures, and subsequently reviewed by them in examinations, is of such a kind that only through the teacher's presentation and exposition can they assimilate it. Such information may either not be conveniently available in, for example, published form; or it may exist in so obscure a form that the pupil cannot deal with it unaided. The second argument is that in any field of study the pupil must master basic principles and general ideas before he can proceed; that in lectures these essentials are presented to him; and that in examinations he demonstrates his mastery of them, or lack of it.

The first of these arguments has some force in the case of history – owing in great measure to the effects of the professional approach. The intense preoccupation of historians with studying the history of their own country on the basis of documentary evidence has resulted in a relative inadequacy of works dealing with other areas. Moreover, as we have seen, the professional approach has encouraged historians to write for a few of each other rather than for their pupils or for laymen. In consequence, many historical articles and books are, quite unnecessarily, so involuted, allusive, jargonistic and intricate in their manner of presentation that only readers who are already familiar with the fields they cover can readily understand their authors' meaning. If it were the case that areas of study other than English history predominate in the history syllabuses of this country's schools and universities, determined lecturers and examiners would have a tolerable argument at their disposal. In fact, this is not so; the argument anticipates the circumstances it would explain, and does not justify current practices. The hard core of most history syllabuses remains the history of England. Amidst the profusion of writing in this field there are, mercifully, to be found enough comprehensible works to meet most pupils' needs. Certainly those needs are distressingly slight, for many pupils at every level are disinclined to acquire by reading information that is supplied them by lecture, in pre-digested form. Yet it remains a poor argument that in effect would justify continued inactivity on the part of pupils by reference to literary ineptitude on the part of historians.

The second argument, for instilling basic principles and general ideas by information-orientated methods, is at once more telling in terms of general theory and more damaging in terms of historians' practice. As the psychologist and educationist Dr. J. S. Bruner has written:[1]

> Teaching specific topics or skills without making clear their context in the broader fundamental structure of a field of knowledge . . . makes it exceedingly difficult for the student to generalize from what he has learned to what he will encounter later.

That kind of information is quickly forgotten by the pupil. But if he has grasped basic principles and general ideas he will be far more likely not only to retain these but also to apply them, and so deal successfully with a wide variety of situations within a field of knowledge: that is, by 'nonspecific transfer'. The notion of 'fundamental structure' is nothing new; similar ideas were central to the celebrated Method of Peter Ramus, critic of Aristotle in the sixteenth century.[2] It presents, however, grave difficulties for historians addicted to the professional approach. They insist upon the particular nature of historical events. They are staunch in their denial of their own ability, or that of anyone else, to draw general inferences from particular historical situations.[3] Consequently, their syllabuses and lecture-courses tend to consist on the one hand of broad surveys that are essentially descriptive, and on the other of close investigations of narrowly-defined and disconnected topics. In neither case are they concerned to demonstrate basic principles and ideas of general application; nor can they argue that historical information is reducible to such a form, and thereby justify their use of information-orientated methods.

[1] J. S. Bruner, *The Process of Education* (1961), p. 31.
[2] See above, p. 23.
[3] Cf. above, p. 38.

The principal explanation for their use of such methods lies elsewhere. It is simply that what historians have chiefly to offer as teachers is their command of information in some particular field of study; and the lecture offers them the greatest opportunity of exhibiting that command without inquiring further into what effective teaching might entail. But there is yet another argument for the information-orientated approach, which invokes considerations of economy in the use of the teacher's time. Methods of teaching other than the lecture are generally held to be excessively time-consuming for the teacher, since they involve him unnecessarily in repetition of what he has to say. Ultimately the validity of the argument depends upon how far it can be shown that the information contained in the lecture must be communicated to every pupil in that form. In the case of history, as we have seen, this is a dubious proposition. Moreover, in view of their liking for lectures it is at their peril that university teachers invoke considerations relating to pupil numbers. Once his material is prepared, there is no limit to the number of pupils whom a lecturer may address in our technological age of audio/visual communications. Certainly it is absurd to pretend that lecture-audiences ought not to exceed numbers implicit in the current staff-student ratio, of approximately 1 to 8 in Arts Faculties.[1] Yet in the interests of preserving a staff-student ratio of this order the universities concur and collaborate in processes of selecting and rejecting candidates for admission.

So far I have suggested that education through the medium of history is poorly served by the information-orientated approach; that amongst its methods the lecture in particular reflects badly upon professional history; and that such methods, which are widely employed in universities at the present time, do not warrant preservation of the current staff-student ratio. I have also suggested, and will in due course discuss at greater length, the relevance of the pupil-orientated approach for teaching history, in the form of gradual study by pupils under individual supervision and in small discussion-groups. Now implementation of that approach does depend upon a favourable staff-student ratio, and so upon selection from among the relatively high number of potential candidates for admission to university history depart-

[1] Source: University Grants Committee (Department of Education and Science Series), *Statistics of Education, 1968, vol. 6: Universities* (1970), pp. xvii, xxi.

ments. It is therefore extremely disturbing that the main instrument at present used to measure candidates' abilities, and so to determine their admission or otherwise, is highly unreliable. That instrument is the essay-type examination. Its weaknesses were demonstrated nearly forty years ago by Hartog and Rhodes, members of the English Committee participating in an international conference on examinations, who singled out for special criticism history examinations both at University Honours and at School Certificate levels.[1] These criticisms drew a spirited response from historians,[2] and the essay-type examination has since been defended on various grounds. But subsequent research has established its deficiencies beyond reasonable doubt.

The examination-situation itself, as we have seen, requires the pupil to behave in a manner that caricatures the way in which I have shown the historian setting about his work. But beyond this, the principal deficiency of the essay-type examination lies in the notorious unreliability of the results it yields. This has frequently been demonstrated in studies that have shown that different examiners arrive at widely different results when they mark the same script, and that a single examiner, however experienced, is alarmingly inconsistent in his results over a series of scripts and over a period of time. Remedies devised for this situation have been mostly statistical in kind: not surprisingly, for the main object of examinations is to enable examiners to express judgements upon candidates in statistical terms. It is a matter for astonishment how cheerfully academics will set themselves up as examiners in ignorance of the elementary statistical precautions that must be taken before their marks can have any validity. Yet expert opinion holds that even when all such precautions have been taken, as no doubt they are by the GCE examining boards, the essay-type examination as an instrument for measuring abilities remains far too unreliable for satisfactory decisions concerning the futures of pupils to be taken on its basis.[3] Much more reliable an instrument for this important purpose is the objective test.

The objective test consists of a relatively large number of

---

[1] P. Hartog and E. C. Rhodes, *An Examination of Examinations* (2nd edn., 1936).

[2] For example, A. S. Turberville and F. J. Routledge, 'An Examination of Examinations', *History*, vol. xx (1936), pp. 320–34.

[3] For example, R. L. Thorndike and E. Hagen, *Measurement and Evaluation in Psychology and Education* (3rd edn., 1969), p. 68.

questions, or 'items', to each of which the candidate responds by choosing his answer from a limited number of alternatives supplied by the examiner. Since marks for every item and every alternative are determined in advance, variation between examiners in marking is eliminated. Even so, this form of examining has provoked a great deal of opposition, much of it more emotional than scientific, and often stemming from defenders of essay-type examination. For example, it has been claimed that the objective test examines only the candidate's ability to recognise a correct answer and does not examine his powers of recall, or memory. The distinction is a doubtful one, for memory is surely involved in acts of recognition. It so happens that the essay-type examination has itself been authoritatively criticised on the grounds that

> The isolation of the student during the traditional three-hour paper may place a premium on unintelligent memorisation, and may tempt him to prepare for it by learning lecture notes by heart for regurgitation in the examination hall.[1]

Thus has much controversy regarding methods of examining sprung from confusion on the part of examiners over diagnosing candidates' mental processes, and confusion over what they themselves are endeavouring to measure. In fact, the range of abilities that can be measured by means of well-constructed objective tests is much greater than is commonly supposed. It includes 'not only the recall of knowledge but also the use of skills of comprehension, interpretation, application, analysis, or synthesis'.[2] But such skills are adequately tested in relation to any field of study only when aims are clearly formulated and basic principles defined for that field. Furthermore, certain important skills are acknowledged to lie beyond the scope of the objective test. These include the candidate's ability in literary composition, and his ability to deal with problems in an original way through the exercise of his own judgement. As we have argued, these qualities are essential for historical study.

The historian is thus confronted with a serious dilemma. I

---

[1] U.G.C., *Report . . . on University Teaching Methods*, op. cit., para. 293.

[2] Thorndike and Hagen, op. cit., p. 103. Such tests, where items are carefully structured in relation to each other and are designed to test specific skills on the part of the candidate by examining his mastery of relevant principles in a field of study, are of course very different from simple tests where every question relates merely to an isolated point of fact.

have suggested on the one hand the desirability for university teachers of history that only a limited number of pupils be admitted to their courses; and on the other, that the method of selection which affords the greatest measure of justice to all candidates does not test relevant abilities. Implicit in this analysis is a further indictment of the professional approach. History continues to be widely taught in schools and in universities in a manner which emphasises the importance of correct information about the objective 'past', and on the basis of writings uncharacterised by literary excellence. In these circumstances, historians have a defective case for resisting the introduction of objective tests for selecting university students. That they do resist such tests while persisting with information-orientated methods in their teaching is a reflection of their failure to apply themselves thoughtfully and seriously to their educational task. Yet to condemn the failings of professional historians is not to solve the present dilemma. In my opinion, it is conceivable that GCE Advanced Level examinations in history might eventually take the form partly of well-constructed objective tests, and partly of 'open-book' essay-type examinations taken over an extended period of time. We have already noted the advantages of the former, but have also recognised their dependence upon adequate definition of basic principles and aims in a field of study. By the latter, several major disadvantages of the conventional essay-type examination are removed. The candidate has access to information other than that which he can recollect in the examination-room; has greater opportunity to organise it and to arrive at a reasoned judgement; and has leisure to exhibit as best he can whatever literary skill he possesses. Examiners, always suspicious of others if not of themselves, are commonly reluctant to relax conditions of supervision and secrecy in the running of examinations, since they fear interference by corrupt teachers and ambitious parents. Yet when both types of examination are run in harness, each can act as a corrective upon the other.

It must be admitted that the problems involved in selecting university entrants are very great. Like the candidates themselves, schoolteachers and examiners have to contend with daunting pressures and frustrations. The obligation is therefore weighty upon university teachers of history to offer all the assistance they can, by striving to make clear what they conceive to be the essentials of their discipline. It is also their responsibility to ensure that when successful candidates at last arrive in universities they find there adequate educational rewards. I do not believe that this responsibility is satisfactorily discharged when teaching is conducted half-heartedly by some form of lecture and again by essay-type examination. Yet these are the methods that have prevailed, and continue widely to prevail, in many university history departments. It is true that in recent years there have been signs of a heightened awareness among some university teachers of their responsibilities towards their pupils, their society and their subject as a medium of education. To a limited extent there have been innovations and experiments in curricula and in teaching-methods, especially in the newer universities.[1] These are hopeful signs. Nevertheless, in my judgement such changes have hitherto fallen very far short of that fundamental alteration of approach to history itself on the part of professional historians in general which I believe to be essential if the place of history within our educational system is to be safeguarded. Nowhere is the absence of such an alteration more evident than in those series of historical publications which have proliferated in recent years, aimed at sixth-form pupils and undergraduates and including contributors from universities of every type.

These publications have taken two main forms. First, there are collections of essays, sometimes 'specially commissioned' and sometimes simply assembled, by several professional historians writing upon different aspects of an historical subject. Secondly, there are collections of documents, each put together by a single historian and accompanied by an introductory essay. Both forms are amply illustrative of the pervasiveness of the professional approach. The prominence given to documents has been revealing enough; it has been interesting to observe how frequently extracts from charters and statutes, treatises and ancient records, have found themselves in print, and how infrequently statistical tables, graphs, models and other analytical tools of the social sciences have kept them company. Again in these collections, professional historians' anxiety to impress each other has very often so far outrun their concern to introduce their material clearly to less practised minds that much of their essays is beyond

---

[1] Though not exclusively there – as I am glad to acknowledge in relation to my own Department.

the grasp of students. But the most disturbing feature of these collections has been their disconnected nature. Despite some ingenuity in inventing titles, and nods in the direction of what one general editor calls 'the doctrine of educationalists', every series tends to consist of separate works resembling each other in little other than format and dealing with subjects between which there is no apparent connection. Moreover, there is all too little to suggest that those volumes which deal with one subject by means of contributions from several historians are the fruit of genuine consultation and collaboration between the contributors. Like the Duke of Mayenne in the last phase of the sixteenth-century civil wars in France, every contributor's overriding concern is with *son particulier*. And the general editors, to whom the responsibility fell of putting these series together, have largely contented themselves with prefatory notes so brief and so cursory that they do not begin to explain how the various volumes in the series relate to the whole, nor what the aims of that whole might be. The overriding impression left by these enterprises is one of continuing concern for autonomy, continuing acceptance of history's fragmentation, and continuing lack of concerted commitment to any clearly-conceived educational purpose on the part of those involved.

It is not by such gestures as these that the place of history in our educational system will be safeguarded. Within that system there is increasing emphasis upon practical usefulness in what is taught. Owing to the professional approach, historians deny what they have to offer in that regard. Yet because their expertise lies in their scholarly command of information upon particular historical topics, they are drawn in their teaching towards information-orientated methods, which are not warranted by the content of history courses. The professional approach dictates the continued preoccupation of historians with traditional areas of study, and prevents the formulation of principles and ideas having transferable possibilities. Professional historians are among the beneficiaries of an educational system that operates on a competitive and selective basis. In such a system there must be sound instruments for measuring abilities. But in the case of history reliable measuring-techniques cannot be applied, partly because relevant abilities lie beyond their scope and partly because historians have failed to agree upon basic principles in their discipline, or even to seek such agreement in collaboration with each other.

In these circumstances it is hardly surprising that history is on the defensive – especially in the schools, where arrows of educational criticism fly more freely and are felt more keenly than in the sheltered world of academics. Educational psychologists have cast doubts upon its relevance. In the wake of studies carried out by the Swiss psychologist Jean Piaget, experiments have indicated the difficulty found by schoolchildren in grasping concepts such as that of historical time,[1] especially when these are laid baldly before them. Their ability to think at the appropriate level is not promoted by their being required, at a key stage in their intellectual development, to absorb large quantities of information upon disconnected historical topics in preparation for their GCE examinations. Beyond temporarily retaining a certain amount of that information, they derive from their study of history all too little intellectual improvement. But methods of examining are so uncertain that such retention is often sufficient to earn them their certificates. In principle history is a very demanding and challenging discipline. In practice it is becoming a soft option. Step by step, headteachers replace it in their schools' curricula with subjects possessing an apparently greater relevance to their pupils' needs.

So history is in decline. Yet the discipline possesses educational potential, of a unique and superior kind. Just as over-specialisation is the weakness of professional history, so is premature and excessive specialisation a weakness of our country's educational system. Had the professional approach not been so great an influence, history might have acted as a powerful counter to the specialising trend. Potentially it affords, as no other discipline can do, a multi-dimensional view of civilised man and his affairs. Potentially it is a cohering discipline: through history, men's multiple activities, past and present, are related to each other, and awareness of those relations made accessible to contemporaries. Of course, its potential can never be realised in full. But such awareness, however partial, must surely involve much more on the pupil's part than compartmentalised assimilation of here some notion about economic affairs, there some idea of religious

[1] J. Piaget, *The Psychology of Intelligence* (1950); R. N. Hallam, 'Logical Thinking in History', *Educational Review*, vol. xix (1967), pp. 183–202.

beliefs, and everywhere a smattering of information about political events. Too often he gains little more than this from his historical studies. But ought not the aim of an historical education to be to equip the student with means of discerning interdependence and interaction in space and time between the many elements of any situation with which he may have to deal? And does not achievement of such an aim depend upon his exercising his judgement by reference to basic principles and general ideas applicable to whatever particular material it may be that may lie before him?

No single historian can hope to formulate such principles and ideas – especially in the present climate of professional opinion, and the present state of history. They will emerge only after historians have acknowledged the *impasse* into which the professional approach has led their subject and them: have acknowledged that history can no longer afford the luxury of allowing every historian to devote his main energies to studying events and situations in isolation from his colleagues. The educational relevance of history depends upon collaborative effort by experienced historians. The range and potential of their subject are of such a kind that historians above all academics ought to seek collaboration rather than competition with each other. It is, of course, in the nature of the subject that basic principles and general ideas, were they formulated, would be neither uniformly interpreted, nor invariably applicable nor unchanging in themselves. But historical judgements are always interim. To declare the impossibility of absolute formulation is no argument against provisional attempts. Such an argument would come close to a denial of the possibility of historical explanation of any kind. Indeed, historians are all too willing to concur – knowingly or otherwise – with those philosophers who, carrying to logical extremes their examinations of the nature of historical explanation, have questioned the admissibility of generalisation in history since no such generalisation can be shown to have the force of a universal law.[1] This alleged difficulty furnishes a further insight into the professional approach, where on the one hand the

[1] For examples, see P. Gardiner, *The Nature of Historical Explanation* (1952); W. Dray, *Laws and Explanation in History* (1957). The arguments of both philosophers, as of others in this field, seem to me vitiated by their reluctance to entertain the dialectical consideration that every generalisation necessarily implies its negative.

historian invokes the aid of auxiliary techniques from minor disciplines to license his investigations while on the other he insists that he himself can deal only with particular events and situations. Thus he renders sterile his scholarly activities and evades his educational responsibilities.

Those responsibilities require historians to recognise that their function as teachers is not to purvey correct information about a limited range of topics which are in any case ever-shrinking fragments of history as the amount of information increases. Their function is to assist the pupil in the exercise of his judgement through furnishing him with points of reference and heightening his awareness by acquainting him with basic principles and general ideas. As a contribution towards their formulation, I will suggest that principles and ideas have distinct roles. Principles may be defined as referents of analysis which historians will recognise as valid in themselves and which they regularly have occasion to employ. Ideas may be defined as referents of suggestion which historians entertain for the insights they afford into historical situations, while recognising that any particular situation is likely to require their modification, reversal or even abandonment. In my view, however far historians may believe in the inductive nature of their studies, all historical interpretation – as distinct from undisciplined accumulation of isolated facts – involves the use of such referents. Let us consider some examples, of a kind relevant to the needs of pupils.

Principles include means of recognising and dealing with verbal problems. In every area of historical study, pupils encounter terms that need to be treated with circumspection. Such terms as 'sovereignty' in political history, 'puritan' in religious history, 'gentleman' in social history, or 'enclosure' in economic history, seem familiar enough. Yet in each case the significance, and indeed the very meaning, of the term varies markedly as it relates to different situations and as it is found employed by contemporaries at different times. Pupils need a general grasp of what such terms may mean. But they can hardly be forearmed against every variation in every occurrence of each one. What they have to grasp above all is an important principle, of inquiring into the contemporary significance of such terms whenever they are encountered. Again, principles include means of recognising and dealing with numerical problems. Especially in studying social and economic matters, the pupil should be equipped to test the validity of numerical argument and made ready to question the evidence upon which such arguments rest. These are arguments which nowadays occur more and more frequently, as historians are drawn increasingly to quantify their conclusions, often on the basis of evidence that is dubious in the extreme.

Ideas may range from large hypotheses approximating to general theory to more specific suggestions concerning relations between aspects of human activity. The teacher should be bold in presenting them, explicit in stating them, as free-ranging in illustrating them as he can be, never allowing them to be submerged by detailed information. The pupil, thus equipped, should apply and test them in limited fields as he studies on his own account and exercises his judgement. Before he embarks upon a study of some particular area of political history, such as that of his own country in certain centuries, his teacher might demonstrate for him in general terms how what is commonly regarded as political activity has directly to do with institutions that are themselves facets of the changing societies they appear to regulate. Again, a pupil who has considered with his teacher broad questions concerning scientific development in a social context may have grasped that most scientific discoveries have not been rapidly followed by widespread training of laymen in their application. A pupil who has grasped this will be prepared to recognise that developments in the science of artillery and ballistics have not usually resulted in prompt improvement in the effective use of guns and projectile weapons. He will now be in a position to understand some important features of military and political history, from late-medieval warfare to the recent Arab-Israeli engagements. Conversely, he will also recognise one reason why Gustavus Adolphus of Sweden, coupling expertise in gunnery with mastery of all technical aspects of generalship, was able to achieve successes that amazed his contemporaries when he intervened in the Thirty Years War in the seventeenth century.

These are merely tentative illustrations. Any historian may suggest as much, and more. Only through serious and concerted effort on the part of many historians, familiar with many different fields and anxious to co-ordinate their expertise, may piecemeal suggestions give way to fundamental structure in historical study. To ascertain basic principles and general ideas would be to preserve a valid place for the lecture in history-teaching. Their precise formulation would facilitate the introduction of more reliable examining-techniques. There would thus be relevance for history in the information-orientated approach, where the content of courses is determined by reference to criteria derived from information itself. But that would be no more than a point of departure, if the educational potential of history were to be realised. For ultimately historical study, and the educational case for history, depends upon the exercise of the pupil's own judgement and the development of his mental powers. We have therefore to ask, what are the mental powers which historians believe their discipline helps to develop?

They often describe those powers by some such phrase as 'the critical faculty'.[1] The phrase has an encouragingly scientific ring; and it is true that an earlier generation of psychologists did endeavour to identify different features of mental functioning in terms of 'faculties'. It is in no way surprising that scholars who rely in their historical studies – which they take seriously – upon a professional approach that has lost whatever relevance it may once have possessed, should rely in relation to their teaching – which they take far less seriously – upon psychological concepts that are obsolete. As the distinguished psychologist Professor J. P. Guilford has remarked, 'Faculty-psychology thinking has been regarded as defunct in psychology for more than half a century but it somehow lingers on in certain educational quarters'.[2] Yet we have noted how in psychological quarters controversy and disagreement persist upon fundamental questions. Thus historians face considerable problems if they are to make their educational case for history in meaningful terms regarding its effects upon the minds of those who study it. These problems are not to be lightly nor easily solved. However, I would suggest that there is relevance for history in the acceptability to many psychologists of a broad classification of thinking into two basic

[1] For example, 'Editor's Foreword' to the volumes in the series entitled *Problems and Perspectives in History* (1964–   ).

[2] G. S. and J. P. Seward (eds.), *Current Psychological Issues: Essays in honour of R. S. Woodworth* (1960), p. 291. Professor Guilford, who of course did not have historians specifically in mind, suggests that faculty concepts may have contributed to the emergence of factor concepts in modern psychology.

modes.[1] While terminology varies, these may be described as, on the one hand, 'convergent thinking' and, on the other, 'divergent thinking'. In my judgement, history affords opportunities for developing both of these; and its potential with regard to the latter endows it with an educational role of peculiar significance at the present time.

Convergent thinking proceeds by assimilation and application of information that is correct.[2] Factual material is retained, and questions are dealt with in terms of their susceptibility to correct solutions when correct techniques of investigation are applied. By contrast, divergent thinking is inventive. Questions stimulate a number of speculative solutions. Any of these may or may not be correct, but they are conceived intuitively rather than by application of standardised techniques of analysis, although such techniques may afterwards apply in testing solutions. Like the distinction between the information- and pupil-orientated approaches which I attempted to draw earlier in this chapter, the distinction between these modes of thinking is not absolute. A capacity for both is no doubt present in all persons of normal intelligence. Divergent thinking is sometimes equated with outstanding creative ability, which implies that the capacity is comparatively rare. But this is not so: intuition is involved in most areas of human activity – and certainly in original work, however modest, in every academic field.[3] Moreover, persons whose intellectual strength lies in convergent thinking are capable of more by way of productive activity than simply assimilating and applying information that is already available to them. By application of correct techniques of investigation they can reinforce and, in some degree, add to the existing store of information. Again, persons of outstanding intelligence may well possess highly-developed capacities for both modes of thinking.

But modern research suggests that in most persons there is an imbalance between the two capacities, and the imbalance is frequently very considerable. Moreover, the information-

[1] Such a classification does not seem to this layman to be invalidated by the differences that exist among psychologists between factor analysts, structuralists and others.
[2] The practical implications are indicated below of the affinity between my definition of convergent thinking and my account of the information-orientated approach (above, p. 92).
[3] Cf. above, p. 100.

orientated approach in education caters for convergent thinking positively at the expense of the other. As I have described it, that approach aims at inculcating correct matters of fact and correct techniques of analysis. Certainly these may be of an advanced and sophisticated kind, making considerable demands upon the pupil's intellect. But the more the pupil's time and energies are engaged in assimilating and applying such material, the less his opportunity for generating and investigating responses of his own in relation to his field of study. Again, the more the teacher is preoccupied with information which he deems to be correct, the less his disposition to recognise the educational validity of divergent responses on the pupil's part. Generally in the modern educational system, persons of high potential for divergent thinking may in substantial numbers be denied opportunity and recognition because the approach most widely implemented within that system, even when it is implemented sensibly and well, does not make adequate provision for those persons' peculiar aptitudes.

While debate continues among psychologists over diagnoses of ways of thinking, I believe that these considerations are significant for history's future educational role. Given an improved foundation in terms of fundamental structure, the discipline would gain in relevance as a medium for developing convergent thinking. Given a contemporary approach as analysed by Connell-Smith, its relevance in a changing world would be far greater. Yet in the public and private situations of such a world, where accustomed practices and procedures so often lack relevance, divergent thinking has an important part to play. Educational psychologists have emphasised the following consideration, if such thinking is to be cultivated by educational means:

> To be well-informed we need only a good memory, to be knowledgeable we must also be able to discover. The merely informed person holds on irrevocably to a once conceived fact. The educated person deals flexibly with presently conceived facts in the full realization that today's fact was yesterday's fancy, and today's fancy may very well turn out to be tomorrow's fact.[1]

I am reminded of a dedicatory remark by a distinguished English historian: 'How can one ever be sufficiently grateful to the person

[1] J. W. Getzels and P. W. Jackson, *Creativity and Intelligence* (1962), p. 127.

who first showed one that all accepted truths, just because they are accepted, tend to become lies'.[1] Yesterday's fancy and today's fact; judgements that are always interim upon situations that are always changing: these we have affirmed to be the properties of history – of history above all other academic disciplines, for no other discipline is so explicitly concerned with these matters as they relate to civilised man and his affairs. To emphasise these properties is to indicate the potential relevance of history to the cultivation of divergent thinking; and so, its special relevance to education in the contemporary world.

How may history's educational potential be realised in practice? There are two methods which, I believe, are especially appropriate and ought to be central in teaching at universities. The first is preparation by pupils of long essays upon related subjects, finally written after extensive inquiry, reflection, discussion and consideration by pupil and teacher together in individual tutorials, with plans and drafts put together from time to time as the work proceeds. Such activity allows the pupil every opportunity to discover, to investigate and to dwell upon numbers of different possibilities arising from the subjects with which he is concerned – most rewardingly when considerations of discovery can be linked with considerations of fundamental structure.[2] I would differentiate very sharply between work of this kind and rapid writing of numerous essays upon miscellaneous subjects directed by teachers operating more or less independently of each other. The latter is normal practice at the present time, is consistent with essay-type examination in its conventional form, and reflects several of its disadvantages. I would also differentiate the method I propose from what is known as 'continuous assessment', where from time to time pieces of work are submitted to be finally assessed before the pupil has completed his course of study. In my view, marks ought to intrude as little as possible upon the process

---

[1] Christopher Hill, *Intellectual Origins of the English Revolution* (1965), p. ix.

[2] 'As much as possible, the learner should take the initiative in exploring and discovering things for himself. Things the learner discovers for himself are rarely forgotten, and it can be confidently expected that their availability in recall will be relatively high, other conditions being comparable. In order to give acquired information transferable possibilities, the information should not be kept in isolation, but should be given connections with other information . . . There is entirely too much learning that limits the information to unit form' (from Guilford's contribution to the symposium *Instructional Media and Creativity*, ed. C. W. Taylor and F. E. Williams (1966), pp. 87–8).

of education; and no final assessment ought to take place until the course has been completed. Assessment by means of essay-type examination in any form raises serious problems, as we have seen; and when important consequences hang upon its results it ought as far as possible to be supplemented by other kinds of testing. At all events, there is nothing to be said for premature assessment; and everything to be said for encouraging cross-fertilisation between related pieces of work in progress. Hence the emphasis I have placed upon continual revision of work as it proceeds.

It is arguable that this method can play only a limited role in schools, where imperatives of selection loom so ominously over teacher and pupil alike, and where the teacher-pupil ratio is not so favourable. The latter circumstance is less a restriction upon use of the second method I would propose, namely the discussion-group. I would again differentiate this very sharply both from the lecture, and from seminars held either infrequently or at best incidentally to other methods of teaching. In the lecture the pupil is unavoidably exposed to a point of view stemming from a single source, namely the lecturer; and this tends also to happen in incidental seminars, however worthy the teacher's intentions may be. The function of sustained group-discussion is to ensure that pupils

> become aware of discrepancies between different people's interpretations of the same stimulus and are driven to weigh the evidence in favour of alternative interpretations.[1]

This requires continuity of membership and regularity of meeting, if diffidence and reluctance to contribute, nowadays exhibited by so many history pupils, are to be overcome. The method is fruitfully employed when, for example, pupils consider together a piece of historical writing or evidence and try to understand

---

[1] M. L. J. Abercrombie, *The Anatomy of Judgement* (1960), p. 62. It is noteworthy that Ranke's own principal teaching method was the *seminar* in which, according to his pupil Sybel, he 'allowed free choice of theme' and 'encouraged each talent to develop along its own lines' (Gooch, *History and Historians in the Nineteenth Century*, op. cit., p. 114). He was also much given to revising his lectures in terms of 'the increased attribution of events to general tendencies, historical forces and principles of development' (H. Butterfield, review of G. Berg, *Leopold von Ranke als akademischer Lehrer, The English Historical Review*, vol. lxxxvi (1971), p. 428). In teaching, as otherwise, Ranke's approach has not been well followed by his professional successors.

and agree upon its meaning. Under judicious guidance they are drawn to recognise the complexities of historical interpretation and can more readily come to terms with the conceptual problems that arise.[1]

Of course, not all pupils respond well to group situations. Some are by nature solitary, or auto-didactic; these are characteristics not infrequently found in the very able. Such pupils are likely to benefit most from personal dealings in individual tutorials with a sympathetic teacher. Opportunities for relationships of that kind are a prime feature of the pupil-orientated approach in education. It is to that same approach that the two methods I have described also belong. But possibly the very able will survive in any case, in any system of education. Indeed, that tautological view is sometimes heard, as an argument against change. Perhaps those who put it forward believe their own survival to be proof of such a view. But in this chapter I am not concerned with extreme cases. Throughout I have been concerned with matters of emphasis. For purposes of analysis I have distinguished between two educational approaches, while stressing that the distinction is far from absolute. No form of teaching can afford to ignore the pupil and his needs. No form of education, however far committed to the pupil, can function regardless of information. In practice, different types of intelligence and different stages in its development merge into one another. What I have tried to suggest is that in schools and universities at the present time there is excessive and unthinking reliance upon the information-orientated approach; that there is poor provision for the pupil and his needs, too little occasion for active involvement on his part, too elevated if unwitting a recognition for convergent thinking, too infrequent opportunity for developing divergent thinking. And I believe the emphasis must be shifted if history is to hold a relevant place within the educational system.

If my analysis is sound, that shift should be away from the information-orientated approach and towards the pupil-orientated approach and its methods. An enlightened balance should be struck between the several methods of, on the one hand, lectures and examinations, and, on the other, individual tutorials, discussion-groups and long essays. The balance should be decisively weighted in favour of the latter three. But changes in

[1] See above, p. 104.

methods of teaching will serve little purpose unless it becomes possible for syllabuses and courses to be coherently planned by reference to agreed and basic principles. Such planning will become possible only when university teachers of history have abandoned the professional approach and have applied themselves to their educational task as their first priority, collaborating seriously and purposefully with each other. Beyond serving the needs of their own pupils, it is also their responsibility to present history in a form appropriate to the needs of their wider audience elsewhere within the educational system. This is not done merely by writing superficial text-books from time to time. Nor is it done by publication of volumes of writings upon particular problems, in series piously believed 'to encourage the development of the critical faculties as well as the memory'.[1] The need is for related materials whereby the pupil himself, through investigating problems on his own account, may grow in understanding of principles transferable to other problems.

My purpose in this chapter has been to analyse history as a medium of education in the light of the discussion we have been presenting throughout the earlier chapters of this book. I have attempted to describe the subject's predicament at the present time, and to suggest guidelines for the future. We have noted how professional historians function within universities which have expanded rapidly in recent years as government and society have made growing educational demands upon them. It is also noteworthy that while this expansion was prompted by a belief in society's need for more scientists and technologists, in terms of student-numbers it has proceeded more rapidly in arts than in scientific subjects. Thus professional historians, whose subject became established in English universities a century ago owing to its presumed relevance as a medium of education, have greatly increased in numbers during the last decade owing again to developments of an educational kind. But they have devoted their main energies to scholarly and esoteric researches, lacking in relevance for anyone but themselves and positively impeding their performance of their educational task. For partly because of the nature of those researches, they have adopted in their teaching an information-orientated approach, while they deny the useful-

---

[1] See above, p. 108, note 1.

ness of historical information and affirm that the subject's educational validity lies in its effects upon the minds of the pupils who study it.

I have argued the relevance for history-teaching of a pupil-orientated approach. Such an approach, and its methods, would justify selection of university students in order to preserve a staff-student ratio which the current approach does not warrant. But if selection-processes are to be equitable, and if history is to be effective as an educational medium, professional historians must make a fundamental alteration of approach to their subject itself. That alteration entails a new determination on their part to collaborate with each other, especially in order that they may discharge their responsibility of defining the essentials of their discipline. But they must also recognise that beyond familiarity with such essentials as a frame of reference, their pupils need maximum opportunity for exercising their judgement and for developing their mental powers. I have indicated that while historians' current notions of the nature of those powers are misconceived, modern psychological research furnishes grounds for claiming that history does have a peculiar educational potential at the present time. Accordingly, I have outlined some teaching-methods whereby, in my view, that potential may be realised.

Of course, I would not pretend that my suggestions afford any immediate and convenient remedy for the current predicament of history. But let there be no mistake over the extreme nature of that predicament, nor over the urgency of historians' task if their subject's place within the educational system is to be safeguarded. It is a task that has been neglected for far too long. Unless it is undertaken promptly, more and more graduates will emerge from our universities having gained from their studies little beyond temporary familiarity with a certain amount of information upon some historical topics. It is difficult to comprehend what society at large can expect to gain from this. There are increasing signs that students themselves find it unsatisfactory. It may be that society's political leaders will persist in underwriting a policy that leads to large-scale production of undermotivated graduates taught by irrelevant methods. In that event, sheer pressure of student numbers may indeed in time deny historians the opportunity for relevant reform. In a situation that promises to become increasingly aggravated, the means of demonstrating in practice the relevance of their subject to education will be taken, gradually but irrevocably, out of historians' hands. Yet for the time being it remains their opportunity and their responsibility to demonstrate the relevance of history.

Conclusion

THIS book has stressed the relevance of history, and has warned of the very real danger that the discipline will decline unless professional historians, who so largely determine the way in which history is studied and written, establish once more its relevance to the needs of contemporary society. And it is a question of *re-establishing* relevance since, for most of the time that men have studied and written history, relevance was among its main characteristics. But professional historians today tend to react unfavourably to the idea that their subject should be relevant. This is because they are heirs to an approach which favours studying the past 'for its own sake'. Yet very many historians appear to be unconscious of the origins of the present position. They are content to specialise in small fragments of history. They tend not to concern themselves unduly with fundamental questions regarding the nature and purposes of their discipline, nor of its practice. Nevertheless, it is possible to identify certain characteristics of what we have called the 'professional approach' to the practice of history: characteristics which do relate to its nature and purposes. We have strongly criticised the professional approach and have urged not merely its modification but its abandonment in favour of a quite different one which, in our judgement, has relevance – as the professional approach has not – to the present circumstances in which the discipline is practised. In this conclusion we want first to set out the essential differences between the professional approach and our own.

First of all, then, we differ fundamentally over the nature of history. The professional approach identifies history with 'the past', and thus sees the historian as a 'practitioner of the past'. The past has an objective existence independently of the historian, whose task therefore is to *recover* it. Since the past survives principally in documents, history is seen basically as the recovery of the past from these surviving materials. We, on the other hand, do not identify history with 'the past', and in any case reject the idea that the latter is recoverable. For us, history's concern is with bringing together the past and the present, and establishing meaningful relationships between past and present situations: or, more precisely, between situations at different points in time, since any division between past and present is an artificial one. This is the historian's *creative* role: the reconstruction of the past in the light of his present circumstances and experience.

We differ no less fundamentally over the practice of history. The professional approach, seeking to recover the past, concerns itself above all with establishing 'the facts'. This, in practice, means the application of technical expertise to documents which are thought to contain those facts. The specialised techniques of historical investigation endow history with its unique character and support its claim to autonomy as an academic discipline. They have also encouraged increasing specialisation and professionalism, and the idea that their application to documents itself produces 'real' history – in the form of learned articles and monographs based directly upon 'original' sources. This 'real' history is written by professional historians for each other, and not for educated laymen. It deals with esoteric subjects and shows an increasing tendency towards jargon and quasi-scientific terminology. A contemporary approach, which we are advocating, involves the reconstruction of parts of the past which have relevance for the historian who undertakes it, and contemporary significance for society as a whole. The mere establishment of 'the facts' about the past is, in our view, a futile exercise for an historian, though appropriate for an antiquarian. The historian's principal asset in his work of reconstruction is the judgement he brings to bear upon the evidence available to him: evidence whose range extends far beyond documentary materials. Thus we reject emphasis upon autonomy, and stress the need for co-operation with other disciplines. History, in our judgement, is an interpretative discipline, relating to each other, in space and time, various other disciplines which in turn relate to different aspects of human activity. We are opposed to over-specialisation which promotes the fragmentation of history; and we believe that history exists not for the training of professionals but for the education – and pleasure – of laymen. Hence we believe that the achievement of literary excellence should always be an important aspiration of professional historians.

Most importantly of all, our own, contemporary approach differs from the professional approach in respect of the purposes of studying history. We reject both the idea that history should be studied 'for its own sake' and the view that the historian's purpose is to establish what happened in the past as an end in itself. History should be studied in the service of society, to meet the intellectual needs of living men and women. Its purpose is to develop judgement and understanding, not to accumulate historical information. In short, we stress the role of history as a medium of education, serving society in this most vital of its concerns. We deplore that considerations of what professional historians judge to be historical scholarship should prevail *at the expense of considerations of education.* Our universities exist both to nurture scholarship and to educate young people. In our changing society the emphasis must be shifted from the former, which has been far too dominant hitherto, to the latter. This cannot be achieved through the professional approach which, as we have seen, stresses historical research positively at the expense of teaching.

Thus we are advocating the abandonment of the professional approach to the practice of history. We have based our argument upon two main grounds: its inherent contradictions and its irrelevance to our present circumstances. We have identified the main contradictions. The most important in our view are those which relate to history and education. They derive fundamentally from the fact that, although history became established in our universities because of its presumed relevance as a medium of education, most professional historians regard themselves essentially as scholars rather than as teachers. This is hardly surprising, since appointment to *teaching* posts is made on the basis of achievement in historical research, and promotion to more senior *teaching* posts is made chiefly on the same basis. As far as their actual teaching is concerned, we have shown how professional historians, who generally stress the only secondary importance of information in historical education, teach very largely by 'information-orientated' methods. In short, the ill-judged professionalism which they bring to matters of scholarship itself induces amateurism in matters of education.

Our second ground for rejecting the professional approach is its irrelevance to our present circumstances, those of a rapidly changing society. We saw in the first chapter the circumstances in which the professional approach developed. In spite of its inherent contradictions, it had some relevance to those circumstances. It is quite inappropriate today. This is partly because of the enormous changes in society since the nineteenth century. But it is also because the masses of documents now available for the study of the past, not to mention other new types of material, have grown so great that the professional approach became obsolete long ago. Those who persist in it wish to arrest the development of the discipline at a point where it was relevant, for that approach still has relevance for them. Indeed, arrested development is an essential characteristic of the professional approach. We saw how, in its origins, it did not go beyond the first stage of positivism, that of establishing individual facts. Detailed research became an end in itself – 'real' history. Many professional historians never extend their researches far beyond the field in which they began their careers; many are content to go over the old controversies regardless of the changing circumstances of their discipline, let alone those of society – from which only too often they seek to withdraw themselves: to 'make a little darkness and call it research'.[1]

As we have observed, there are signs that some historians are not unaware of the *impasse* into which the professional approach has led their subject and them. Eminent members of the profession have issued warnings. Gestures have been made, however inadequately, in the direction of educational reform.[2] No less an organ than *The Times Literary Supplement*, announcing that

the most serious problem confronting history today is a fragmentation and an arid professionalism which, if given rein, will rob it of relevance and meaning

believes that 'Happily the younger generation of historians is well aware of these dangers'.[3] We do not share this optimism. The professional approach, in our judgement, remains all too great an influence upon historians of every kind. Some of the 'new ways in history' proclaimed by the *Supplement* are evident in the views

[1] R. H. Tawney, quoted in Postan, *Fact and Relevance*, op. cit., p. 56.
[2] See above, pp. 47, 102–3.
[3] 'New Ways in History' (7 April, 1966), p. 295.

recently expressed by the Economic and Social History Committee of the Social Science Research Council. So too is the professional approach. That Committee reviewed 'some of the most important aspects and problems of research, bearing in mind in particular the needs of non-specialists, rather than the interests of professional economic and social historians'.[1] It stressed the limitations of 'the classic Rankean discipline of historical investigation'. It observed how British historians have lagged behind many of their colleagues abroad in adopting alternative methods of investigation, and showed how disappointing has been the British contribution to research upon foreign and international subjects. It recognised 'a minor renaissance in social history' and attributed this partly to 'the fact that so many contemporary concerns close to the personal experiences and preoccupations of writers and readers do in fact lend themselves to an historical approach'. It called for better collaboration between historians and between disciplines. In short, much of the Committee's review is in harmony with criticisms and suggestions which we ourselves have made. And yet, two features of that same report illustrate all too clearly how reluctant historians remain to make that fundamental alteration of approach which we believe essential if the future of history is to be safeguarded.

First, the report made clear[2] how dissatisfaction with the methods and approach of professional history has prompted economic and social historians to affirm the distinctiveness of their fields of study as branches of the social sciences in their own right, and to dissociate themselves from established university history departments. The territory of 'real' history is thus eroded even further, and the discipline's fragmentation rendered even more extreme. But secondly, the influence of the professional approach remains strong upon these would-be social scientists. Despite its general recognition of the importance of 'contemporary concerns' for historical work, the Committee soon lost sight of this consideration when it evaluated particular areas of study. Regarding the 'early modern period', for example, it declared with some satisfaction that owing to recent work

[1] Social Science Research Council, *Reviews of Current Research: Research in Economic and Social History* (1971), p. xi. Subsequent quotations and statements from this report in the remainder of this paragraph are drawn from pp. 17, 8, 119, 15, 18, 125–6.
[2] Ibid., pp. 1, 128.

It is now possible to discuss in far more fruitful ways the relationship between social structure and economic processes, the determinants of critical variation in population and production, and the very nature of Britain's preindustrial economy.[1]

Will such discussion assist 'non-specialists' towards a better understanding of the nature and problems of underdeveloped economies in the contemporary world? Is such an understanding likely to follow from study of *Britain's* pre-industrial economy? Is that area of study judged to have special potential for yielding understanding in general terms of the extremely important social and economic problems identified by the Committee? Or has it received so much recent attention largely because enough relevant documents have become available to keep historians in 'technological employment'? The Committee did not pursue such questions as these. For its members, it was evidently enough that historical discussion be enriched for the benefit of academics.[2] And in order that enrichment may proceed apace, they announced that historians 'need relief from normal academic duties if they are to maintain research "productivity" '.[3]

In our judgement, the duties of academics have been sacrificed for far too long upon the altar of research. In the case of history, we advocate reappraisal of priorities and purposeful recognition and pursuit of the subject's relevance as a medium of education above all else. We deplore the professional's self-image, whereby he sees himself as a member of a small, self-sufficient and self-perpetuating élite devoted to the pursuit of learning and interpreting that pursuit in esoteric terms. We believe that such an attitude is harmful not only to history but ultimately to society at large. As long as professionals reserve 'real' history for themselves and their main energies for its study, they will effectively continue to deny their contemporaries the benefits that might accrue from a truly contemporary approach. We have noted how laymen appear to be interested in history, and how history has long been established in the political arena. If professional historians continue to shrug off their wider responsibilities towards their subject, others will continue to exploit it at the expense of history

[1] Ibid., pp. 93–4.
[2] See especially ibid., p. 128.
[3] Ibid., p. 127.

and of society alike. Most important of all, we consider the professional's self-image to be a wilful self-delusion. For although professional historians regard themselves not as educators but as scholars, they owe their existence in their present numbers mainly to the fact that history is widely taught throughout our educational system. It is taught by teachers practised in professional ways, and on the basis of materials supplied by the professionals themselves. In the setting of our schools and colleges, history is prominent among those examination-subjects that provide the basis for processes of selection which have very serious effects upon the lives of young people. The wider responsibilities of historians are thus far-reaching and inescapable. Professional attitudes, rejecting the present for the sake of 'the past', imply a desire to minimise and to evade them. Our own advocacy of relevance implies an ambition to discharge those responsibilities to the full.

We welcome the challenge inherent in the present situation. Unlike those who persist in the professional approach, we believe in the importance of history's potential role within our society and within our educational system at the present time. Society is undergoing bewildering change. It is hag-ridden by experts, confused and harassed by over-ready application of piecemeal and hastily-formulated solutions to deep-seated and interrelated problems. For such a society we believe in the relevance of a discipline concerned with cultivating not technical expertise but reflection and mature judgement upon many-sided and multi-dimensional human problems. The educational system, it is widely recognised, suffers from barriers of over-stratification and over-specialisation. There is too little communication between its several institutions at their various levels, too little contact between different disciplines and even between members of single disciplines. In history, by the approach we favour, there is unique potential for lowering these barriers. History alone embraces every area of human activity. It is capable, as Gibbon recognised long ago, of appealing to every intellectual level. When historians devote themselves to promoting coherence and not fragmentation, collaboration and not autonomy, communication and not expertise, general issues and not particular ones, human and not technical values, there will be no doubt of the relevance of history, and no question of its decline.

INDEX OF PERSONS